PUSH ON

MY WALK TO RECOVERY ON THE APPALACHIAN TRAIL

NIKI RELLON

with

Jeremy Elvis Herman

SANNWALD PRESS, INC.

Push On: My Walk to Recovery on the Appalachian Trail
by Niki Rellon with Jeremy Elvis Herman

Copyright © 2018 by Niki Rellon
NikiRellon.com

Published by

SANNWALD PRESS, INC.

ISBN 978-1-7320540-0-4 (softcover, color)
ISBN 978-1-7320540-1-1 (softcover, black and white)
ISBN 978-1-7320540-2-8 (eBook)
ISBN 978-1-7320540-3-5 (Audio)
Library of Congress Control Number: 2018901198

Editing by: Jeremy Elvis Herman
Cover Design by: Niki Rellon, NikiRellon.com
Interior Layout by: Nick Zelinger, NZGraphics.com

10 9 8 7 6 5 4 3 2 1

1. Memoir   2. Nature Travel   3. Motivational

First Edition 2018

Printed in the United States of America

This book is dedicated to all the people who made my
walk to recovery possible:

To the EMS, and the surgeons and nurses at the Hospital in
Grand Junction and the Hospital in Denver, who kept me alive.

To my family and the staff at the rehab facility back in Germany,
who helped me to get back on my feet.

To all the prosthetists in Germany, in Austria, and especially in the
US, who made it possible to hike 2,200 miles on a prosthetic leg.

Thanks to all the incredible people I've met on all my journeys
throughout the world.

Special thanks to Paradox Sports, to all my sponsors,
and to the people who donated to my fundraiser.

Thanks to all the trail angels and hikers I met during my AT hike.
You made my thru-hike possible by giving me the
encouragement and motivation I needed to push on.

Niki Rellon,
The "Bionic Woman"

"Only those who risk going too far can possibly find out how far they can go."

~ T.S. Eliot

CONTENTS

> "When we are no longer able to change a situation,
> we are challenged to change ourselves."
> ~ Victor Frankl

For Jin

from the
"Bionic Woman"

Niki Dillon

1

FREE FALL

Click.

Oh Scheisse!

I knew immediately that something was terribly wrong.

That click—the last time I'd heard such a sickening sound was when my right shoulder dislocated during free fall while I was skydiving. The force of the wind pushing up against the injured joint was agony, but I didn't have time to dwell on the pain. I also couldn't afford to let the misery cloud my judgment. If I reached over with my left hand and pulled the ripcord handle on the right side of my body, my parachute would have wrapped around me like a burrito. I would have struck the ground with enough force to shatter my bones and explode my organs. Fortunately for me, I remembered my training, and I pulled the auxiliary ripcord on my left side. The reserve parachute deployed perfectly, and seconds later, I landed outside of the drop zone in a horse pasture.

The landing threw me on my butt. I wanted to sit there for a moment, so my heart could settle down, but a dozen well-fed horses were galloping right at me. I was sure they were going to trample me to death, so I jumped up to my feet. To my relief, they stopped just before they reached me. Then they did something curious: They trailed after me as I tried to collect my parachute. I've heard that horses are quite intuitive. I wondered if they were following me out of concern. Maybe they sensed that I was in excruciating pain.

That story ended very differently from this story. I walked away that time, thanking my lucky stars. But this time I wasn't so lucky, and I didn't walk away.

Celebrating a smooth jump and a safe landing

November 1, 2013, started out as a cold day, but that wasn't unusual for autumn in Utah. I woke up at 4 a.m. with seven other adventurous souls ready to begin our canyoneering trek through Montezuma Canyon. We'd driven down the night before, so we could get an early start, knowing that it would take the whole day to get through that magnificent canyon. I didn't really like waking up before dawn, but we wanted to be sure we exited the canyon before sunset. Safety first!

Montezuma Canyon bragged a 250-foot drop on the back end. Rappelling down the near-vertical rockface should have been the exciting finale of our day, and then we should have had an hour-long, straightforward walk out of the canyon to our car. But things didn't exactly go according to plan that day.

Before we headed into the canyon, we checked our own gear. The ropes were sound. The anchors and neoprene suits checked out. The backpacks were all full. So, we ventured in, certain that we had everything we needed for a successful day. In hindsight, I shouldn't have been at all confident in my harness.

In other sports like scuba diving or skydiving, we always check gear for each other, but that morning we didn't double-check each other's harnesses, maybe because canyoneering is a relatively new sport and no routine has been established yet. The harness I'd used previously had been an American-style harness, but it was long gone, taken by my ex-boyfriend when we broke up and split up our belongings. The one in my backpack on that cold November morning was a European-style harness, and I'd never used one like it. The French guy who'd sold it to me, Louis, was one of the canyoneers traveling with me that day. He'd given me a quick lesson in how to use it, but it's clear to me now that I should have asked more questions. I should have insisted that he explain more thoroughly how it worked. I know this sounds ironic, but I probably would have been more careful if I'd had less experience. When I was a beginner, I double and triple-checked my gear before doing anything dangerous. But here I was getting ready to rappel down a canyon as tall as a giant sequoia with a harness I'd never used, and I'd only asked a couple questions. I had just enough experience to have developed a false sense of security. It just goes to show you that there's a fine line between confidence and carelessness.

As the sun rose over the horizon and warmed our chilled bones, the electric buzz of enthusiasm energized the group. The day was shaping up to be spectacular, and we chatted and joked like eager kids on a school field trip. I was drawn to one of the canyoneers, Sabrina, a German chick who shared my love of Jägermeister (a.k.a. German medicine). She was new to the group, but we quickly bonded over discussions about our childhoods in Germany. She volunteered to carry my camera, so she could take pictures of me throughout the day, and I asked her if she'd be my backup on that final descent down the canyon. We were well on our way to becoming good friends.

After an hour and a half of walking, we stopped to put on our neoprene suits, so we wouldn't freeze our butts off when it came time to swim. This Meetup group advertised itself as a crew that loved "spectacular adventures," and they were keeping their promise.

We spent more than eight hours hiking, swimming, and climbing before we arrived at the brink of the canyon wall. I was practically giddy as I dug my harness out of my backpack. We all geared up, then the most experienced members of the group drove the stainless-steel anchor bolts into the granite stone. I was fourth in line, so I didn't have long to wait to rappel down that intimidating red-brown rockface.

11/01/2013 13:05

Minutes before I free fell the final forty-five feet of a 250-foot rappel

As soon as I pushed off, I knew I had a serious problem. I was spinning round and round like a carousel. 360 degrees, 360 degrees, 360 degrees. Blue sky, brown canyon, blue sky, brown canyon, blue, brown, blue brown. Faster and faster, over and over again. I was twirling out of control, and I was quickly descending toward the craggy bottom of the canyon. I panicked, and my breathing became heavy. Knowing that I had to stop these rotations, so I could determine what had gone wrong, I pulled on the rope as hard as I could. About forty-five feet from the bottom, I finally stopped spinning like a fishing reel. And then I heard a sickening sound: *click*.

Moments before I heard that "click"

Suddenly I was in free fall, and I saw the rope flying unattached above me, my body plummeting toward the unforgiving ground below. It would take me less than 2 seconds to fall those final 45 feet, and I'd be traveling at 50 feet per second in the instant before I hit the ground. I like free falling I'm a skydiver but without a parachute?! I screamed: *Scheisse! I don't want to die!* I screamed so loudly that my throat ached, and my solar plexus burned from the fear of death. Then the world faded to black as I lost consciousness.

Those people at the bottom of the canyon who could see me watched helplessly as my harness came completely unattached from the belay rope. Sabrina, who was my safety person, couldn't see me from where she was standing, so she didn't know what was happening. She continued to pull down on my rope, just as she was supposed to.

I was unconscious when I collided with the earth, my left foot first. I'm probably lucky that I was insensible when I crashed onto the rocks; if I'd stiffened in anticipation of the impact, I might have shattered every bone in my body. The collision shocked me back into alertness.

I landed facedown with my head pointing downhill. The canyoneers at the bottom rushed to my aid. Gasping for breath, I told them not to worry about taking precautions to safeguard against spinal cord damage. If they didn't turn me over and move me up the hill so I could fill my lungs with air, they would soon be performing CPR compressions on me.

As they picked me up and repositioned my broken body, I could hear the fractured bones of my pelvis scraping against one another. Crepitus, I've discovered, is infinitely worse than the sound of fingernails on the chalkboard or a dental drill boring through enamel. I had experience as a paramedic in Germany, and I took EMT basic training as a ski patroller here in the US, so I knew that I needed a tourniquet around my pelvis to prevent internal bleeding. I weighed 143 pounds (65 kilograms), which meant that I had four to five liters of blood in my body. Unless they acted quickly, I could bleed out in less than forty-five minutes.

After they turned me and set me back down on the ground, I felt an excruciating pain in the center of my back. I wondered how my friends could be so stupid as to set me down on a sharp rock. I'd later learn that the broken vertebra in my back was the source of that pain. Twelve broken ribs, a fractured sternum, a collapsed lung, a mangled middle finger, a shattered pelvis, and a splintered leg were the source of the countless other pains that were tormenting me.

The adrenaline that had flooded my body during the fall was quickly receding, leaving me in unbearable pain. It was pain like I had never known before, pain that to this day, I can't really describe to other people. It was so horrendous that it prevented words from escaping my lips. It covered me like an unwelcome blanket. The pain was so severe that I nearly broke the fingers of whosever hand I was squeezing for comfort. The pain seemed to last forever. I thought it would never end, or that it would end me.

Squeezing a hand for comfort

"Some people think to be strong is to never feel pain. In reality, the strongest people are the ones who feel it, understand it, and accept it."

~ Unknown

All seven of the people who were with me whipped out their cell phones to call for help, but no one had service. It would have taken an hour to walk out of the canyon, but I probably didn't have that long. Someone suggested that they check for boats on Lake Powell, which wasn't far from where I'd fallen. Jeff, one of the canyoneers, raced down to the lake with an emergency whistle in his pocket. He spotted a boat not far from shore and blew his piercing whistle as loud as he could. Shouting and gesturing, he somehow communicated our need for urgent help. That boat passed the plea on to a second boat, the second boat alerted search and rescue, and search and rescue called for a helicopter. It wasn't long before I heard the whirl of helicopter blades, but the sound soon faded. There wasn't enough space to land in the canyon, so the pilot set the helicopter down about a thousand feet below me. The nurse and the paramedic sent to save me had to hike up to where I lay.

Landing spot for the first helicopter, 1,000 feet below where I lay   Nurse and paramedic hiking to my location

While I waited for help, I squeezed the hands of my fellow canyoneers—one after the other—to cope with the agony that stripped me of the ability to think straight. Every couple minutes, the person whose hand I was crushing pried off my fingers, and one hand was substituted for another. To their credit, they didn't complain. They willingly submitted to my vise grip in the hope of offering whatever small consolation they could in an unreal situation.

After what felt like an eternity in hell, the nurse and paramedic, who had to hike that steep canyon wall, finally arrived. They immediately gave me morphine, which was blissful relief from the misery, then they stabilized me on a spinal board. I don't remember everything from this stretch because the drug has blurred my memory, but I do recall being told that a second helicopter had landed about an hour and a half after the first one.

Nurse and paramedic finally arrived

I remember being loaded into the second helicopter, which had one landing skid halfway in the air because the pilot couldn't find flat ground to put down both skids.

After they crammed me into the smaller chopper with no room for anyone except me and the pilot, we flew to the rendezvous spot, where they transferred me into the larger helicopter.

The pilot and I on the way to the rendezvous spot

I remember distinctly a conversation between the pilot and the nurse. The nurse told him that she wanted him to fly to the hospital in Grand Junction, Colorado, but he said he couldn't.

"My air time's up," he explained. "I can't fly all the way to Grand Junction. I have to call another pilot to relieve me."

"If you don't fly Niki to Grand Junction now, she'll die on us. Is that how you want to end your day?" she replied.

That's interesting, I thought. *I'm dying.*

It took a few minutes of arguing, but the nurse eventually convinced the pilot to fly directly to Grand Junction. I was quite impressed with her stubbornness. I guessed that she had some German heritage.

Finally on the way to the hospital

"Here is a test to find whether your
mission on earth is finished.
If you're alive, it isn't."
~ From *Illusions* by Richard Bach

2

BAD NEWS
FROM THE SAWBONES

On the morning of November 1, I was in perfect health; by evening of that same day, I was lying in an operating room in Grand Junction, yelling at the orthopedic surgeon who wanted to amputate my left leg.

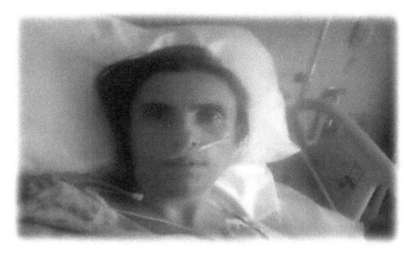

Emergency room in Grand Junction, Colorado

"It's broken beyond repair," he explained, handing me a consent form on a clipboard.

"No way in hell you're cutting off my leg!" I yelled.

"You'll never be able to walk on it unassisted. At least with a prosthetic leg, you won't need a crutch or a cane."

"You don't understand," I argued. "I'm an athlete. That's what I do. If you take my leg, then I'm nothing. How would you feel if someone told you that you couldn't be a surgeon anymore?"

"You can still be an athlete with a prosthetic leg. Look at all the—"

"You're not listening!" I interrupted. I was worked up, and my collapsed lung and broken ribs and sternum were making breathing difficult. "You're not taking my leg! If you do, then you might as well just ship me off to Switzerland. Suicide's legal there, you know."

A corner of his mouth curled up, and he said, "No need to go all the way to Switzerland. It's legal in Oregon too, and it's a lot closer."

"I'm glad you think this is funny!" The adrenaline was pumping through my body.

He held up his hands in surrender. "OK, OK. I get it. No amputation today. We'll do what we can."

"With everything that has happened to you, you can either feel sorry for yourself, or treat what has happened as a gift. everything is either an opportunity to grow, or an obstacle to keep you from growing. You get to choose."
~ Wayne Dyer

I went into surgery wondering how this had happened. Just hours earlier, my body had been in great shape, strong and whole. I'd become a world champion kickboxer and a European champion boxer with this body. The first time I traveled to North America from Germany, I'd ridden my bicycle more than 15,000 miles over a two-year period, from Alaska to Mexico City, up and down both coasts, and across the country. In 2006, I hiked from Mexico to Canada along the Pacific Crest Trail, a 2,600-mile journey that took me six months to complete. I was an avid triathlete, a scuba diver, a skier, a windsurfer, a skydiver, a canyoneer, a kayaker, a cyclist—the list goes on and on. I'd used my body to do things that most people save for bucket lists, and now I was being told that I'd be lucky if I ever walked again without a crutch. What was I supposed to do, get an office job? Settle down? Give up everything I knew?

I woke up the next morning with a tube down my throat. The first thing I did was to look down at my left leg. An external fixator held it together, and a suction pump was sticking out of the sole of my foot, but at least it was still there.

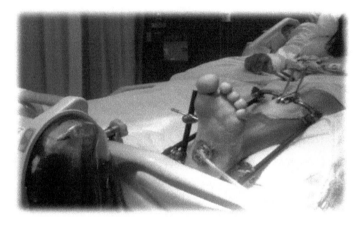

The morning after the accident with a leg fixator and suction pump after surgery

I had refused to comply with the surgeon's wishes, so he operated on it rather than amputating it. I told myself that I'd prove him wrong, that I'd learn to walk again without a crutch. Hell, I'd learn to run again. I'd do whatever it took to get back to one hundred percent, or at least as close as humanly possible.

I also had a fixator attached to my pelvis, which had been broken so badly that it was upside down and splayed out like an open book. The surgery required a specialized technique to ensure that the pelvis was aligned perfectly, and only a handful of surgeons can perform the operation. Fortunately for me, one such surgeon had been on call that night at the hospital in Grand Junction. That was one piece of good luck in an otherwise unlucky day.

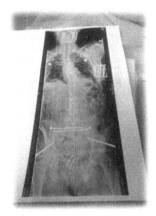 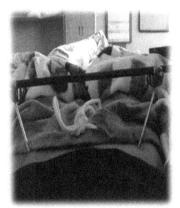

Naked and all screwed up   External pelvis fixator

Some of my canyoneering friends showed up that morning to find out how I was doing and to express how thankful they were that I was still alive. Because I was intubated due to a collapsed lung, the only way I could communicate with them was with a blackboard. But even that wasn't easy given that the middle finger on my writing hand was broken and I was drugged up on morphine. I asked Sabrina, my new German friend, to contact my parents back in Germany. They speak very little English, and she proved to be a huge help. She also called my landlord in Denver, terminated my month-to-month lease, and arranged with some of my other friends to have my belongings moved into my camper van. I owe my friends so much for all they did for me during this harrowing time in my life.

I was still intubated four or five days after I came out of surgery, which meant that I couldn't talk with anyone or eat solid foods. When the time came for the tube to be removed, I was both relieved and frightened. I hadn't breathed on my own in days, and I hoped that my collapsed lung had healed enough to work without assistance. While the doctor removed the tube from my throat, the nurse gave me a dose of tough love.

"You'd better start breathing on your own, Niki! Or we have to put that tube right back in!" She yelled at me the way a trainer yells at her client at the gym.

Determined to talk and to eat again, I fought desperately to suck air into my lungs. I had a massive coughing fit while the doctor stood next to me ready to stuff that horrible tube back down my throat. After what seemed like an eternity, I finally felt the sweet relief of air flooding into my lungs. Ahhh! I was able to breathe again. It was a step toward independence.

Respiratory therapy began that same day. They gave me a plastic device attached to a tube that I had to suck on until a purple ball floated to the 500-mL mark. The goal was to get that ball up to the 1,000-mL line eventually. I also received oxygen therapy for about fifteen minutes twice a day.

I spent three weeks stuck in my bed in intensive care in Grand Junction. No trips to the bathroom. No visits to the cafeteria. And the closest thing I got to a shower in all that time was the day a nurse washed my hair with some sort of powdered shampoo.

After four weeks of hoping against hope that my left foot would heal, a doctor finally showed me an x-ray. All the bones were shattered, making it look like a jigsaw puzzle. The tibia and fibula were also completely disconnected from the ankle. The doctor who had told me that it was damaged beyond repair had been right. It would never heal properly. Staring at the image of my demolished foot, I finally realized that amputation was probably my best option. If they'd shown me that x-ray on the night I came in, I might even have agreed to the amputation then.

One of my canyoneering friends is a doctor, and he helped me get in touch with a specialist surgeon in Denver, my hometown. Dr. H. coordinated with the staff in Grand Junction Hospital to have me transported to Denver, where I'd spend the next three months of my life.

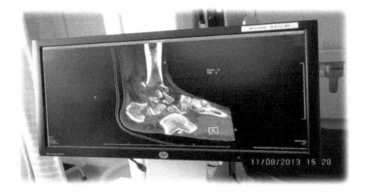

X-ray of my shattered foot

On the afternoon I was to be transferred, the helicopter that was scheduled to take me to Denver was diverted on an emergency call, so I had to wait until the helicopter was available. It eventually showed up, and I arrived in Denver that night. After the helicopter set down, they wheeled me into a room that wasn't much more than a glorified box. I quickly fell asleep, and I'd only been out for a couple hours when a nurse woke me up—I think it was around 2 a.m.—to ask me my weight and height. I was angry that she'd interrupted my rest for something so unimportant, and I grumpily replied that I weighed 63 kilograms and that I was 1.71 meters tall. She was dumbfounded by the numbers. When I explained that I was using metric measurements, she asked me what metric was. I felt like I'd walked into a Third-World hospital, and I wondered if it had been a mistake to leave the Hospital in Grand Junction

At 5 a.m. that same morning, I had to use the restroom, which was impossible for me to do on my own. I pressed a button to call for assistance, and in walked the nurse who'd somehow managed to graduate from nursing school without learning about the metric system. When I asked her for help, she barked at me like I was a naughty child trying to shirk her responsibility.

"All patients have to use the toilet on their own," she said with her arms folded in front of her chest.

I looked at her in disbelief. "Do all patients have fixators in their legs and their pelvises?" I shot back at her. "Do they all have broken spines and ribs and sternums?" I glared at her spitefully. "If you make me pull myself out of bed, I'm probably going to fall and break something else. And then you're going to have to explain my new injuries to the doctors."

My rant did the job because she helped me to the restroom, but the scowl on her face made it very clear that I wouldn't be able to rely on her for assistance in the future.

Later in the day, a staff doctor apologized for the hiccups and for the nurse's poor behavior, explaining that they hadn't realized that I was arriving so late and they weren't prepared to meet my needs. My surgeon, Dr. H. also came by to introduce himself. He's one of only a small number of surgeons in North America who can perform the Ertl Bone Bridge Procedure, and after we talked, he scheduled the amputation of my left leg below the knee for November 30, just a few days before my thirty-ninth birthday. He would fuse the tibia and fibula together using the technique that had been developed in 1920 by Professor Janos Ertl, Sr., a Hungarian surgeon who made it his life's mission to give amputees a chance to live a pain-free life. His procedure has helped countless people around the world over the past century, and Dr. H. convinced me that it could help me as well. So, hand shaking, I put my name on the consent form. My hope for a full recovery was gone, as if it had bled out of the pen that I'd used to sign away my left leg.

One of my friends, who was one of the canyoneers who witnessed my accident, showed up at the hospital the day before the surgery. He and a nurse put a coat of polish on the toenails of the foot that soon wouldn't belong to me. It was a living, pulsing part of my body, but in less than a day, it would be a dead lump of inert matter. I started to wonder what would become of it. Would they toss it into an incinerator with other useless limbs and organs? Or would they dump it into a biomedical landfill? I hated the thought of strangers carelessly discarding something that had been so important in my life.

That foot had helped me kick my way to the top of the kickboxing world. It had pedaled me across the country and carried me from Mexico to Canada along the Pacific Crest Trail. I wanted that foot, and if I couldn't have it attached to my body, then I at least wanted to have the final say in how it was disposed of. I asked Dr. H. if he would save it for me after surgery, and he agreed to put it in a freezer, so I could do with it as I pleased. I also requested a spinal block, so I could remain conscious during the amputation. He wasn't at all receptive to that idea.

"This isn't Disneyland," he said, shaking his head.

On my bicycle tour through North America from 2002 to 2004

The night before surgery, I lay in my bed thinking about how drastically my life was about to change. I was going into the operating room with two feet, but I'd come out with only one. The free-spirited life I'd known was over. I'd no longer be an adventurer who could pick up at the drop of a hat and travel the world in search of new and interesting experiences. I wasn't just losing a limb; I was losing my identity. I'd be a completely different person when they rolled me out of that OR. The thought made me sick to my stomach. I felt like everything was collapsing around me like a house of cards.

"Everything is hard before it is easy."
~ Goethe

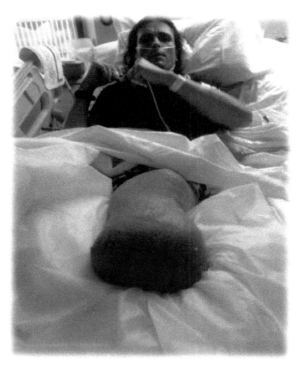

After my below-the-knee amputation surgery

I've always been a person with an eye toward the future. When I'm not hiking mountains or sailing seas, I'm researching and saving money for my next big adventure, my next grand challenge. But when

I came out of surgery with a missing limb, I couldn't picture myself in the future. I could only think about what I'd done in the past, and what I'd likely never do again. The long bicycle tours that had taken me all over the country, the hikes that lasted for months, the motorcycle trips that took me up to Alaska and down to Key West—they were all things I'd done in the past. The new me would have to content myself with looking back on those experiences with a mixture of pride and sadness, the way that we look through photo albums that contain memorable moments from our past.

It wasn't just the treks and the trips that I'd miss. There were also work opportunities that would no longer be available to me. In order to become a US citizen, I'd spent nine years wrangling with the governments of the United States and Germany, and I paid around $10,000 in government and legal fees. When an attorney friend finally helped me become an American chick, I decided that I wanted to join the Navy Reserve, so I could work as a paramedic in the military, which would also help me get a loan to buy a piece of property in Alaska and maybe a sailboat. With that vision for my future in mind, I'd started taking college classes to prepare for the Armed Services Vocational Aptitude Battery (ASVAB) test. But now I'd never be a reservist. I'd also considered finding work as a ski patroller or a ski instructor, and I had connections that could have opened doors for me. But now those doors would slam shut. Everything I imagined doing involved two legs, and now that I only had one, there was nothing out there for me, at least nothing that didn't involve pushing a pencil behind some desk.

While I lay on my back in that hospital, I sank into a deep despair. The hospital staff obviously recognized the signs of depression because they placed a guard outside my door to ensure that I didn't try to take my own life. They also sent visitors to my room one after another to cheer me up. Some of those people were psychologists, but even at my happiest, I'm not receptive to what shrinks have to say. (Maybe some of them I believe they became shrinks, to heal themselves).

Others were patients who walked in on prosthetic legs to show me what my life could be like if I could just push on through this dark spell. And my friends dropped by often to encourage me to stay positive. On one occasion, they kidnapped me out of the hospital and took me to an indoor rock climbing event that featured amputees tackling the wall. Now I appreciate what everyone did for me during that bleak stretch, but at the time, I wished they'd all go away and leave me to my wallowing.

The kidnapping crew that took me to a rock climbing gym during my hospital stay

While my mind was ailing, my body was mostly just numb, owing to the morphine that the hospital staff pumped into my veins to help me manage my pain. During the first couple weeks in intensive care, I was too drugged to function normally or to care about much of anything.

I started physical therapy shortly after my amputation surgery. A couple days into PT, one of the therapists approached me about mirror therapy. Phantom pain in an amputated limb is one of the chief concerns for an amputee, and for certain people, the most effective way to cope with the pain is to trick the brain into thinking that the leg is still there. Mirror therapy involves placing a mirror between an amputee's legs, so the healthy leg is reflected in the mirror, which creates the illusion that the amputated leg is still attached to the body. For fifteen minutes a day, the amputee moves the healthy leg while simultaneously imagining a symmetrical movement in the amputated limb. Many amputees report a significant reduction in phantom pain with regular mirror therapy.

Until that point, I hadn't had any phantom pain, but I assumed that the therapist knew what she was doing, so I sat down and did everything she told me to do. Later that day, I experienced phantom pain for the first time. It was excruciating. It felt like my foot was on fire, which was ironic given that my leg was in a freezer somewhere in the hospital. The pain was so severe that I might have been tempted to find the nearest sharp object and cut the damn thing off if someone hadn't already beaten me to it. When I talked to a doctor that night, I found out that an amputee who isn't experiencing phantom pain shouldn't do mirror therapy because it can actually trigger the pain. Some therapist!

That wasn't my only bad experience with a physical therapist. A few days after my encounter with the mirror therapist, another therapist nearly caused an accident that undoubtedly would have sent me back into the operating room. Part of my daily routine in therapy involved using crutches to walk around a square block in order to prevent atrophy in my healthy leg. One afternoon I saw a scale and decided to see how much less I weighed without my left foot. I used my crutches to step up to the scale, which was about ten inches off the ground. After I saw the number—by the way, amputation is great for weight loss!—I told the therapist that I was ready to sit back down in my wheelchair. I reminded her several times that day to lock the brakes on the wheels, so the chair didn't roll as I tried to sit in it, and I assumed that she'd taken my reminders to heart and set the brake. But when I grabbed the chair and began to sit, it started moving backward. The remainder of my core strength allowed me to pull myself forward to prevent my already ailing body from crashing to the floor. I have no doubt that a fall would have caused untold damage to my broken back and pelvis, not to mention to my ribs and sternum. When I finally managed to climb into the wheelchair, I screamed at the therapist, telling her that I never wanted to work with her again. I didn't complain about her when I saw a doctor that day, but in hindsight I probably should have.

When Dr. H. visited me the next morning, he said: "You are in the dog house" (with the therapist). She had the gall to complain about me!

"Telling the truth and making someone cry
is better than telling a lie
and making someone smile."
~ Paolo Coelho

Not long after that run-in, they removed my intravenous pain pump and transferred me to oral painkillers. To my surprise, they gave me a medication called Marinol, which is made from cannabis. They also prescribed OxyContin to help me manage the nerve pain.

The OxyContin did a great job of blunting the burning and electric-shock sensation, but I became so constipated that at one point a nurse had to use her gloved fingers to remove everything from my rectum. That was definitely one of the most humiliating moments of my life.

I wasn't in much of a mood to celebrate on the day I turned thirty-nine years old, but the staff did their best to make the day memorable for me. My favorite nurse, Jeanne, asked me what I wanted for my birthday. I jokingly told her that I was craving some liquid bread. We Germans love our beer, I explained, and I hadn't had one for more than five weeks. She arranged to get two bottles of IPA from my favorite microbrewery. They were 12% alcohol by volume, and after I chugged them, a huge grin broke out over my face. I took to the hallways in my wheelchair, popping wheelies in front of the nurses' station.

Only in Colorado can you get stoned and drunk in the hospital on your birthday.

12% beer on my birthday in December   Marinol high

3

SO LONG, SAWBONES

After nearly two months in the Hospital in Denver including five weeks of inpatient rehabilitation at another facility, I was kicked out. Staying at the hospital was costing a ridiculous amount of money every day, so the bean counters decided to transfer me to a charity hotel. I'd still receive daily physical therapy at the Medical Center, they assured me, but I'd do it as an outpatient. I told them that I didn't think I was ready to leave. In fact, I begged them to let me stay longer. I still had a fixator attached to my pelvis, and I had an IV line in my arm for the antibiotics that I needed to fight off an infection that had landed me back in intensive care for several days shortly after my amputation (they wanted to give me a blood transfusion because my hemoglobin level was low, but I didn't want to risk getting some disease, so I refused. I'd already received 1.5 liters of blood right after my accident, and I didn't want to push my luck). But my pleas fell on deaf ears. They sent me off on a pair of crutches and a temporary prosthetic leg that had weight restrictions. I gimped out the front door with my pride smarting and my body hurting.

Hospital transportation to and from the hotel was unreliable, so for the next few weeks, I had to limp through early spring slush to get to the hospital and then back to the hotel for my physical therapy sessions. It was only about a mile each way, but it felt so much farther in my hobbled condition. I was always exhausted when I arrived.

When I first got to the charity hotel, a nurse met me with a thirty-day supply of antibiotics. After she taught me how to administer the drugs into my IV line, she told me that I had to do it myself while I stayed at the hotel. Because I had paramedic training, I wasn't intimidated by the process, but I was shocked that they were asking me to push my own antibiotics. That can be tricky for someone who has no medical background.

Not that a medical background is a guarantee that the nurses and doctors won't make serious mistakes. One morning while I was at the rehab facility, I noticed a red pill in the little white medication cup that a nurse handed me. When I asked the head nurse why I was getting new meds, her face went white and she put her hand over her mouth to cover her shock. They'd accidentally given me another patient's meds, a guy who'd just had heart surgery. I dodged a bullet that day because I could have very easily gone into cardiac arrest if I'd taken the meds from that other patient.

I have to admit that a tiny part of me welcomed the move to the Charity-hotel because I'd grown tired of staring at the same four walls day after day, and I liked being in a place that didn't smell antiseptic, but I was mostly just terrified of what was to come next. I had no job, no apartment, little money, and a disability that would make it difficult for me to acquire a job, an apartment, and money. I was seriously worried that I might end up on the streets, and this was in early spring, not exactly the ideal time to sleep in my camper van. Even if I hadn't been in pain so severe that I cried most nights, sleep would have been hard to come by. As I lay in bed at that hotel, my mind raced from one depressing scenario to the next.

But then something amazing happened. Just days before I was scheduled to be discharged from the hotel, someone from Paradox Sports contacted me to inform me that they'd held a CrowdRise online fundraiser on my behalf. The news stunned me. I'd never even heard of Paradox Sports, but they'd heard my story from a base jumper who'd been at the same time in that Hospital in Grand

Junction I'd been there. He was skydiving with a wingsuit, he crashed into a mountain, breaking his ankle so severely that he nearly became an amputee, as well. They'd raised enough money to put me up in an apartment for three months!

After I finished talking to a manager from Paradox Sports, I sat down and researched the organization. I discovered that they're a nonprofit that specializes in "adaptive outdoor recreation." Based in Boulder, Colorado, they provide trips, trainings, and community outreach for people with disabilities so they—I should say we—can continue or start participating in mountain-climbing activities. After the disbelief wore off, I reached out and thanked them again and again for what they'd done, but I don't think they'll ever know just how meaningful their gesture was for me. Those weeks at that hotel were among the lowest of my life, and I'm not sure what would have happened to me without their help.

My camper van and my motorcycle

I left that Charity-hotel nearly four months after my fall, and I found a month-to-month room to lease in a house in Denver. The rent was outrageous for a single bedroom, and I had to share the place with three roommates, but that was a hell of a lot better than sleeping in my camper van in freezing conditions. And, besides, I didn't plan on staying for long. I was determined to use my time there wisely, to plan my next steps carefully so I wouldn't be in such a bleak situation again.

Shortly after my accident, some of my friends had moved all my belongings from my old month-to-month apartment to my van. I didn't realize until I went to my van to collect my things on move-in day that they'd saved the gear I'd been wearing the day I fell. The helmet, the elbow and knee pads, the harness—they were all there in a box. I immediately tossed that damn harness into a dumpster. I hated looking at the thing because it reminded me of how stupid I was to buy it. I could have bought a new one from REI for about $45, but I bought a used one for $25. I nearly died because I wanted to save less than the cost of a burger and a beer at Chili's.

I'd had some conversations in the hospital with some of my canyoneering friends, and we came to the conclusion that somehow the carabiner was clipped into the non-weight-bearing webbing that orients the leg loops rather than into the belay loop. I'd gotten too comfortable with rappelling, and I failed to double-check the system. I typically double-check my gear the night before an outing, but the weekend before my fall, I'd left my harness in the truck of one of my canyoneering friends. I grabbed it from his truck at 4 a.m., right before we started out on our early morning hike, and I didn't double-check it. Really, I'm lucky the harness didn't fail sooner. I'd spun my way down 200 feet before I managed to stop my body from spinning. My abrupt halt caused the synthetic band to tear all the way through, separating my carabiner from the harness. I'd only fallen forty-five feet. If I'd fallen even an extra fifteen or twenty feet, I probably wouldn't be writing this story right now.

My mouth dropped in awe when I picked up the helmet I'd been wearing that day. I'd worn it for five seasons as a ski instructor, which meant that it had kept my head safe for more than 500 days. But now there was a huge crack right down the middle of it. I'd broken my body in dozens of different places, but I didn't even have a headache after the fall, thanks to that helmet. My careless brain had caused all the injuries that my body sustained, but the head that housed that brain escaped unscathed because the helmet had sacrificed itself for me. I think often about that terrifying crack in the plastic dome.

Seeing the helmet didn't upset me the way that seeing the harness did, but I still threw it out. I didn't want to spend any more time dwelling on my past mistakes. I'd only cause myself regret and heartache. I wanted to start a new life, to figure out how to move past all this pain. So, in the trash it went, along with everything else that reminded me of that day.

"Don't worry about failures; worry about the chances you miss when you don't even try."
~ Jack Canfield

I moved all my belongings from my camper van into a house that felt a lot like a college dorm. I took a couple days to set up my room and put away my stuff, and then I headed to a physical therapy center for intensive neuro-rehabilitation. Learning how to walk properly on my prosthetic leg so that I wouldn't need crutches wasn't just a matter of figuring out the fit of the socket on my stump. The learning process was complicated by the nerve damage caused by the break in my pelvis. The physical therapist was supposed to help me get back on my feet, literally and figuratively, but I didn't have a positive experience with her. In fact, if I listened to her advice, I might be rolling around in a wheelchair today.

One session with her was especially disheartening. To gauge the damaged nerves in my lower body, the physical therapist stuck needles up and down the backside of my legs, from my glutes to my quadriceps.

This reminded me of an experience I had back in 2002, when I was riding my bicycle along the Pacific Coast Highway. I stopped in Venice Beach, a residential neighborhood in Los Angeles, and while I was on the boardwalk, I saw a comedian standing in front of a small rug covered with broken glass. He spotted me standing in the crowd and asked me if I'd like to get on his shoulders while he walked over the glass. After handing my bike off to a bystander, I climbed on, and he walked over several feet of broken glass.

Each time the physical therapist inserted another needle into my flesh, she asked me what I felt. I wanted to tell her that I felt like the fakir walking over the broken glass, but she was always so somber, and I knew she wouldn't appreciate my sense of humor.

"I don't feel anything," I told her instead.

"You have severe nerve damage," she replied. "You probably won't ever be able to contract your quadriceps enough to bear your weight. I don't think you'll ever be able to walk again without crutches. You should think about getting a nice wheelchair."

I was livid with her. She should have been trying to motivate me, not trying to discourage me. I appreciate honesty from medical professionals, but I also know that it's never appropriate for a physical therapist to tell a patient that she can't do something when the therapist knows nothing about the mindset of the patient. I'm a strong-willed person, and her statement made me determined to prove her wrong. But what happens to a person who believes the physical therapists when they say that something is impossible? The mind is capable of amazing feats of healing, but it can only help the body when it believes in itself. I wonder how many amputees out there have settled for life in a wheelchair because some pessimistic physical therapist gave bad advice.

Fakir with his rug covered
in broken glass

Walking over broken glass with
me on his shoulders

Not long after I started physical therapy, I decided that I needed to get back into shape. My muscles were used to being stressed and abused, and they were crying out for real exercise. I quickly settled into a comforting training regimen. I started swimming with a local swim team; we practiced together three times a week. I also found free yoga classes at a facility that trains yoga instructors. The studio was only a few miles from where I lived, and there were several sessions every day. On top of all of that, a team from Paradox Sports invited me to climb with them at an indoor rock climbing gym. I got a great workout at that gym once a week.

Indoor rock climbing gym in Denver

In the beginning of April, I received my permanent prosthetic, an extra-lightweight, carbon-fiber work of art. It was so much more functional than the test socket that I had in the beginning. It was also beautiful. I loved the Grateful Dead image that wrapped around the socket that fitted over my stump. I can't say that I'm a huge fan of the band, but that picture of the skeleton with the rose-covered skull has always been one of my favorite pieces of pop art. And now it has extra significance for me. Every time I look at it, I'm reminded of my brush with death and the impermanence of life.

Besides giving me a new leg to get around with, my prosthetist also helped me customize my bicycle. He shortened the pedal for my left leg, which drastically improved the bicycle's performance. I used it to get all over Denver. The only time I drove my camper van was when I needed to buy groceries.

My prosthetic socket

Before becoming an amputee, I never appreciated how tough feet are. Because we spend a lifetime walking around on them, the skin on the soles of the feet of even the laziest people can hold up under significant force. But the skin that was now holding up my weight inside the socket of my prosthetic leg was as delicate as a newborn's foot. It wasn't used to supporting 140 pounds of pressure, and it became very tender to the touch after just a couple hours of walking. It took a few months for my stump to toughen up enough so that I wasn't in pain when I walked. But I had to be careful not to push the scar tissue too much, and I had to keep it slathered with an ointment meant to prevent it from opening again, which could have led to another infection. I'd taken various antibiotics to that point, and I was concerned that my body might develop a resistance to them, so they'd no longer be effective. I had to walk a fine line between pushing my body and protecting it.

I also had to learn how to tweak the socket of the prosthetic to minimize friction. To fill space inside the socket, I had to wear several layers of cotton socks. Sometimes I had to add socks, while other times I had to remove them. In the mornings, my stump was usually swollen, and I had to take socks off, so it would fit into the socket. But when the swelling decreased several hours later, I had to add socks to prevent the stump from rubbing against the socket. It took a lot of patience to figure out a system that worked for me.

I had to visit my prosthetist regularly, so he could adjust the prosthetic with an Allen wrench, shave off bits here, add pieces there, change the volume. Fine tuning and tensioning requires a lot of trial and error, and you can't know if your latest modifications were good or bad until you've put some miles on the leg. In those first few months out of the hospital, I came to value the work done by prosthetists. Their training requires knowledge of physics, kinesiology, human anatomy, and mechanical engineering. On top of all of that, they must be trained as counselors in order to work with people who are going through a life-altering change.

The endorphins that my body produced while I exercised helped me cope with the negativity I was encountering at that Rehabilitation Hospital, but they did nothing for my wanderlust or my adrenaline addiction. Just a couple months after I moved into that rental house, I began to get antsy for an adventure. Like a nomad, motion is my bliss. Nothing makes me happier than waking up in one place and going to sleep someplace totally different. If I'm stuck in one spot for too long, doing the same thing over and over again, I feel trapped. But my bank account was running on fumes, and I was still a shadow of my former self. Where could I go on a shoestring budget? And what could I do that wouldn't over-stress my body?

As if in answer to my questions, my brother called me one day from Germany. He was getting married to his girlfriend, and he wanted me to attend their wedding. Of course, I'd come, I told him. I wouldn't miss his happy day for anything. Except…I couldn't exactly afford a plane ticket to Germany right then. I couldn't even afford my rent right then. But he was my only sibling, and he had a baby daughter I'd never met. One way or another, I'd figure out a way to get to Germany.

A couple days after that conversation, I remembered my friend Maryanne, who works for Delta Air Lines. In the past, she'd offered to set me up with a buddy pass, which allows friends and family to fly—standby—at a substantially reduced rate. I called her up and told her that I wanted to arrange for a flight from Miami to Germany.

"Don't you live in Denver?" she asked.

I told her that I planned to ride my motorcycle across the country before I left for Germany. I thought the long trip would be a great challenge, and it would be a much-needed escape from my dull routine.

"Are you out of your mind?" she asked, sounding a lot like my mom. "You lost your leg how many months ago?"

"About five and a half," I told her.

"And now you want to ride halfway across the country?"

I told her that I was done with the doctors and physical therapists at that Rehab-Hospital. They weren't doing anything for my body that I couldn't do by myself, and they were actually worsening my mental state. I got nothing but negativity from them. I wouldn't be able to do this, they told me. I should give up on doing that. They insisted that I get comfortable with the thought of spending most of my time in a wheelchair. They always painted such a bleak picture of my future. Where was the color? Where was the hope? Rather than helping me fight my way back to wellness, they mostly just pushed drugs on me. I'd met another amputee who'd lost his leg around the time I'd lost mine, and he told me that he was taking more than ten pills a day. If I'd taken the advice of my doctors, I probably would have been taking about that many as well. In fact, one doctor went so far as to forbid me from weaning myself off the pills I was taking for my nerve pain, but I quit them anyway. I knew better than to let them talk me into getting hooked on pain meds. I did take an occasional OxyContin when the pain became unbearable, and I took Tramadol when the pain was more moderate, but that was only a fraction of what they wanted me to take.

"I know it sounds crazy, but I know what I need right now," I told her. "And it's not another mom."

"OK. No more nagging. I promise. But if you change your mind, just let me know and I'll get a ticket for you out of Denver whenever you want."

"A great pleasure in life is doing what people say you cannot do."
~ Walter Bagehot

Soon after our conversation, I gave notice to the crazy landlord who wouldn't let me keep my coffee maker on the kitchen counter. When I told him, I was leaving the country for a while, he made it very clear that I wouldn't be welcome back in his rental after I returned to the States. I didn't think that was such a big loss, but he acted like I'd thrown away the opportunity of a lifetime. He also refused to return my deposit. I had to show up with a muscle-bound friend to get it back. What a creep.

After paying Maryanne for the plane ticket, I didn't have enough money to stay in hotels along the way, but I was a pro at pitching a tent at the end of a long day of travel. Cycling all over North-America for two years helped me discover all sorts of creative ways to find free camping spots. I also thought it would be good for my muscles to set up and take down a campsite every day. And riding that motorcycle would strengthen my knees and quads, my core, my shoulders and neck. It would also force my mind to purge all the unhappy thoughts that had accumulated over the past several months. When I'm on my motorbike, I don't have the luxury of wallowing in self-pity. I have to think about the road conditions, the flow of traffic, the highway signs. I have to focus intently on the here and now, which was something I hadn't been able to do with any success since my accident. This would be a step in the right direction for both my physical and mental health.

On my motorcycle

4

BACK IN THE SADDLE

Before I left Denver, I decided to take another motorcycle safety class. I signed up for a steeply discounted two-day course, but when the owner of the school, a professional motorcycle racer, found out that I intended to ride my motorcycle across the country so shortly after my amputation, he told me that the class was free. What a deal! I was the only person who enrolled, so it was just me and the instructor for both days. He had me drive around cones, ride over obstacles, and practice quick safety stops. I ended up becoming friends with the instructor, and we rode to some incredible spots around Colorado before I departed for Miami.

I packed up and jumped on my bike about two months before my brother's wedding. I intended to take my time getting to Florida. Besides strengthening my body and healing my mind, I wanted to visit some of the friends I'd made while riding my bicycle all over the country. I also wanted to enjoy the ride. If my travels have taught me anything, it's that the journey is usually more fulfilling than the destination.

"One of the happiest moments in your life is when you find the courage to let go of what you can't change."
-Unknown

I didn't get far before I had mechanical problems. Just before arriving at Colorado Springs, the Pingel Enterprise electronic shifter on my handlebar went kaput. A prosthetic leg can't flex downward to shift gears on a motorcycle, so I had a handlebar shifter installed before leaving Denver. It allowed me to shift with my thumb rather than with my foot. It should have made my life on the road significantly easier, but I had issues with it almost immediately after it was installed. I'd had to have it towed to a repair shop on three separate occasions before I left Denver, but I wouldn't have left for Miami unless I was fairly certain that the mechanic had finally fixed it that third time.

From Colorado Springs, I took a detour to the Valley View Hot Springs, a nature sanctuary a couple hours southwest of Denver. It boasts soaking ponds, wilderness trails, geothermally heated hot tubs, spring-fed swimming pool, rustic accommodations, and naked people everywhere you look. Valley View Hot Springs is a clothing-optional sanctuary. It's not a place for the shy or the prudish.

Valley View Hot Springs camping site

I spent a couple days there soaking my battered body and sleeping in my tent. While I was enjoying one of the hot springs, I met another motorcyclist named Charles, and we decided to ride together to his friend's place to visit another hot spring. Halfway to Paonia—it's the opposite direction of Miami, in case you're keeping track—my motorcycle died on me. Lucky for me, I had jumper cables, and Charles gave me a jump-start. I was able to make it to his friend's place in Paonia, but I couldn't shift at all. I got smart this time and had the tow truck take me to a specialized Colorado Springs dealer. I paid through the nose to have the shifter repaired—thank God for credit cards—but at least the problem was finally solved. Or so I thought.

From Colorado, I rode down to the Montezuma Hot Springs near Las Vegas, New Mexico. These springs are right next to the highway, which means that you can just pull over, hop off your motorcycle, and climb into one of the three tiny pools. The water was really hot, like lobster-boiling hot, and it felt great after a long day on my bike. But by the time I crawled out of the springs, my limb was swollen, and I couldn't squeeze it into my socket. No biggie. I'd just crash in my sleeping bag next to the hot springs, get a good night's rest, and push on the next morning. Wishful thinking.

Shortly after I zipped up my sleeping bag, a security guard from the World College University across the river showed up at my camp-site. He told me that the college oversaw the springs, and he informed me that camping was not allowed in the area. I explained my situation to him and showed him my swollen limb, then he left without saying a word. I assumed that meant that he understood my situation and was giving me a free pass. But forty-five minutes later, I saw red and blue flashing lights on the shoulder of the road. What the heck?! The security guard hadn't even the decency to ask me to leave. He just walked away and called the police. Jerk. The cops were far friendlier than the security guard, and they listened intently as I explained about my swollen limb. They took mercy on me and didn't write me a ticket, but they told me that I had to leave immediately. Fortunately for me, the swelling of my limb had subsided some, and I just barely squeezed it into the socket. I thanked the officers for understanding my predicament, then I climbed on my bike and went in search of a peaceful camping spot for the rest of the night.

I made it to Texas before the next issue arose. As I was pulling into a gas station to fill up my tank, flames started shooting out of my handlebar. My beloved motorcycle was on fire! At a gas station!! I grabbed the bucket of water meant for cleaning windshields and doused the flames. Holy moly, that was close!

I was in the middle of Nowhere, Texas, and, once again, I no longer had a fully functional shifter. I had to manually shift my poor motorcycle into third gear before leaving the gas station. Riding for several hours with a roaring engine on the interstate, I managed to get to some Podunk town in Alabama, where I met up with a pair of adventure riders I'd met online. We shook hands, then immediately went in search of a motorcycle repair shop.

The adventure riders, Jeff and Sally, were an awesome couple, and they let me stay overnight at their home. The following morning, the mechanic gave me the bad news: he couldn't fix my bike because he had to order specific parts from overseas, and delivery could take months. I was upset, but Jeff, who owned several foreign motorcycles that he repaired on his own, told me that the mechanic was full of baloney. He towed my bike back to his house and got to work on it. After a thorough inspection, he determined that nothing was wrong besides the electronic shifter. All I needed was a simple replacement part. I had it overnighted from Pingel Enterprise, and because the shifter was still under warranty, I didn't have to pay for anything, not even for the cost of shipping. Jeff installed it the next day and told me that the issue was completely resolved. I hoped he was right, and so did my family. Every time I posted something on Facebook about a breakdown, they got more and more nervous about me making it to Germany in time for my brothers weeding.

From Jeff and Sally's house in Alabama, I rode all the way to Florida with no problems. There weren't many red lights and traffic wasn't heavy, so I rode almost the entire night without needing to shift. About 125 miles north of Miami, I pulled into a gas station to buy a cup of coffee and to take a short break. I sat on the lawn next to the gas station, and I immediately fell asleep, coffee cup still in hand. When I woke up, I saw a woman peeking at me from behind the corner of the gas station. She seemed strange, so I figured I'd better get back on the bike and push on. As I started the engine, she ran toward to me and grabbed my handlebar to prevent me from leaving.

"I called the cops on you!" she yelled.

"Why'd you do that?" I shouted back over the engine. "I didn't do anything wrong."

"There's no sleeping on the premises!"

I tried calmly explaining that I hadn't meant to fall asleep and that I'd only taken a quick power nap, but there was no appeasing her. So, I resorted to nastiness. I cranked on my throttle in neutral to make the engine sound like a roaring tiger, and I told her that if she didn't immediately release my handlebar, my emotions were going to redline, and she was going to have a pissed off biker chick on her hands. That finally did the trick. She let go, and I was on my merry way.

> "One life. Just one.
> Why aren't we running
> like we are free?"
> ~ Unknown

I arrived in Miami six weeks after I left Denver. I called my friend Maryanne straightaway to tell her that I'd finally made it. I'd met her more than a decade ago, while I was bicycling all over North America. Her son, who is also a cyclist, had been riding back to Miami from

Key West when we met on the highway one afternoon. We got to talking about our long-distance cycling experiences, and before we parted ways, he gave me his mother's address in Miami and suggested that I stop by her house as I bicycled my way back through The Magic City. I spent the winter in Key West working in a restaurant as a chef, but I eventually headed north again and visited Maryanne in her home. We've been good friends ever since.

Working as a chef in Key West, Florida

She invited me to her downtown apartment. It had an incredible view of the Atlantic, and we watched a magnificent sunset while eating sushi on her balcony. Then we talked about my motorcycle adventure, which she'd been tracking on Facebook. Like my parents, she'd been worried that I wouldn't be able to make it to Miami before my scheduled departure date.

At some point, our conversation turned to the HMS Bounty, which I'd sailed on as a deckhand for about a month back in 2002. Maryanne broke the news to me that the ship had sunk about ninety miles southeast of Hatteras, North Carolina, on October 29, 2012.

Hoping to move the three-masted, 180-foot vessel out of the path of Hurricane Sandy, the sixty-three-year-old skipper who'd commanded the ship for seventeen years, left port and sailed it out into the Atlantic. Massive waves knocked out both ship's generators, and without them the bilge pumps couldn't dispel the water that was quickly pouring in from all sides. After a prolonged battle against the hurricane, the Captain ordered all hands to abandon the ship. Fourteen crew members were saved by the Coast Guard, but the Captain and a relatively inexperienced deckhand were both lost at sea. It was a sad end to two lives and to a magnificent ship that I'd loved.

"Ships don't sink because of the water around them; ships sink because of the water that gets in them. Don't let what's happening around you get inside you and weigh you down."
~ Unknown

Back when I was cycling from Alaska to Key West in 2002, I stopped off in St. Petersburg to visit the Salvador Dali Museum. I spent an afternoon admiring paintings from my favorite artist, then I went for a ride along a pier, where I stumbled upon the HMS Bounty. My jaw dropped. I'd seen the 1984 remake of Mutiny on the Bounty back when I was still a kid—this Bounty had been built for the 1962 version of the movie—and I'd fallen in love with that beautiful ship. I'd dreamed about sailing around the world on the Bounty, and here she was in the flesh, so to speak.

I was studying the Bounty intently when I discovered a small, wooden sign posted near the ship. The words on the sign were almost completely obscured by crusted bird crap. Curious to know what it said, I uncapped my water bottle from my bicycle and washed off the white foulness. My heart started pounding when I finally saw the sign's message: "Deckhand for hire. Low pay, good food, opportunity of a lifetime." What?!

The Bounty in St. Petersburg, Florida, in 2003

Without a moment's hesitation, I locked up my bicycle and mounted the gangplank to search for the captain. I was going to get this job, no matter whose arm I had to twist or palm I had to grease to get it.

I poked my head into several cabins before I finally found someone.

"Can I help you?" asked a middle-aged guy sitting behind a desk.

"Maybe," I said doubtfully. "I'm looking for the captain."

"You found him."

"Oh," I said, immediately regretting the disappointment that I could hear in my voice. He looked nothing like the person I imagined at the helm of the Bounty. He wore a green polo shirt, ill-fitting khakis, and wire-frame glasses. He looked more like a nerdy middle manager at an accounting firm than the captain of my dream ship.

"I know, I know. I'm not what you expected. No wooden leg. No bird on my shoulder. No cutlass hanging from my hip."

"No, it's not that…" I stammered. "I just…I saw the sign about the deckhand. Is the job still open?"

Captain of the Bounty

"We've got one more spot to fill."

I tried to keep myself cool, but a ridiculous smile spread across my face. "I've got to have that job. I'll do whatever it takes to get it."

"You ever sailed before?" he asked.

"No," I admitted, my smile dimming a bit, "but I'm a quick study, I'm a damn hard worker, and I'm stronger than most men."

"I can see that." He looked me up and down. I felt like he was sizing me up like I was cattle at a livestock auction. "Can you be ready to ship out in two days?"

My overly enthusiastic grin returned, and I said that I was "Born ready."

He shrugged. "OK, then the job's yours."

My eyes became saucers. "Really?" I asked dumbly.

"You might not be so happy in a week. The work's hard, and most landlubbers puke their guts out all day every day until they get their sea legs."

"Can I ask one small favor?"

"Sure."

"Can I bring my bicycle with me?"

"Yeah, no problem. We've got plenty of room onboard."

So, we shook hands, and I was officially employed as a deckhand on one of the last few tall ships on Earth.

On my first day aboard, one of the crewmembers showed me the engine room, which doubled as the sleeping quarters for four unlucky deckhands, including me. It was unbearably loud, and it stank like feet and dirty underwear.

Just a couple days earlier, I'd camped out on the beach, where I was lulled to sleep by the whoosh of waves at night and awoken in the morning by the skree of seagulls. With that peaceful—and pleasant smelling—image in mind, I went on a mission to find a better place to crash at night. On the sunshine deck, I discovered a safety boat that I decided to make my bunk. I loved the idea of waking up to incredible sunrises and the feel of the wind on my face. Not long after we set sail, I shuffled up to the safety boat after finishing my night patrol, around 4 a.m., and I discovered another crewmember sleeping in my spot. I kicked his butt out and told him never to invade my space again. I must have scared him because I never saw him in the boat again.

Me in my sleeping spot in a safety boat on the Bounty

As a newbie, I had to climb up the mainmast ahead of the other nine crewmembers to prove my worth as a shipmate. The first time I did it, I climbed up the rope without shoes. Every step I took, the rope burned into my feet, and I nearly shit my pants in fear as I approached the top of the 111-foot mast.

There were moments during that first climb when I thought I'd gotten in over my head, but my ego refused to allow me to turn back, knowing that the other nine crewmembers who were following closely behind me would lose respect for me. I wish I could say that I was relieved when I made it to the top that first time, but it was terrifying to be eleven stories above the deck of the ship with nothing more than a belt around my waist attached to a rope by way of a carabiner.

Climbing up to
the mainmas

Enjoying the view 111 feet
above the deck

I looked out at the glorious view of the ocean, but I could only enjoy it for an instant. We had work to do. Part of my duties as a deck-hand included taking care of the sails, which meant that in addition to stitching up the holes, I had to help unfurl and set the sails. When I reached the top of the mast, I inched my way out over the left yard of the topsail—that's the horizontal spar that runs perpendicular to the mast. Because I was the first person to the top, I had to scooch over to the very end of the yard. At the end of the mast I was not standing with my hip against the mast, but with my quads, which made balancing quite tricky.

The waves rocked the ship up and down and side to side, and I felt like I was sitting on a rollercoaster. Thanks to my love for extreme sports, I'd had a lot of experience with situations that would make the knees of the average person knock, but this was almost too much even for me. My terrified brain was screaming for me to climb down to safety, but I had to ignore its demands and see to my duties.

I'm taking a pause to enjoy the sea air

When all the crewmembers were in place, we pulled up the topsail. The boatswain piped his commands to ensure that our efforts were synchronized.

"One, two, three topsail up. One, two, three topsail up."

Over and over again we pulled the ropes until the topsail was up. Then I had to make some complicated seaman's knots. I definitely would have screwed them up if the woman next to me hadn't helped me. Once all the other sails were also up, we climbed down to the deck. I was thrilled to have survived my first challenge on the Bounty.

Crew on the yard of the mainmast, bringing up the topsail

After we left St. Petersburg, Florida, we sailed down to Dry Tortugas National Park, due west of Key West. Then we sailed up to Georgia, where I left the Bounty to continue cycling up to New York City. I was onboard for about four weeks, but those are four weeks I'll never forget. The businessman who owned the Bounty made it his mission to give people the opportunity to learn how to sail on one of the world's last remaining tall ships. I'm lucky to count myself among those who had that chance.

I had dinner at Maryanne's apartment in downtown Miami, then we started our drive to her boyfriend's apartment in Ft. Lauderdale. I intended to follow her car on my motorcycle, but when I tried starting it up, I discovered that the battery was dead again, thanks to that damn shifter. We charged up the battery, and I followed her to Ft. Lauderdale. I decided that I was done fighting the bike, so I left it in her boyfriend's garage until I returned from Germany. I didn't want to waste any more time dealing with it before my plane departed.

Getting ready to leave the Bounty in Georgia to continue
my bicycle journey to New York City

The next morning, I borrowed Maryanne's car and drove to some secondhand clothing stores to find something nice to wear, both for my flight and for my brother's wedding. Maryanne told me that my disability made it likely that I'd get bumped up to first class, but only if I was dressed in business casual attire. I hate shopping, especially for fancy clothes, but I loved the idea of flying across the Atlantic in first class. So, I went hunting.

I found the perfect dress at the first store I visited. It was dark purple and had cute sparkles. More importantly, it was only $45. At an antique store right next door, I found another great deal on a wedding gift for my brother and his soon-to-be wife. A couple years earlier, they'd rented a car and driven along Route 66 from Chicago to LA, so I bought them a framed Route 66 picture to commemorate their journey. I was done in less than an hour. If shopping were always that easy, I probably wouldn't hate it so much.

My new dress from a
secondhand store in Miami

The present for
my brother's wedding

I left for Germany the next morning. Just as Maryanne predicted, Delta upgraded me to first class. I was thrilled that I'd get to spend seven hours in a big, cushy seat. This was one of the few times since my accident that my prosthetic leg was an asset rather than a liability.

Once I was in the air, I felt a jumble of emotions. The last time I'd visited Germany—for paramedic training—I'd stayed in Berlin at the tiny garden house I'd owned for years. But I'd had to sell it because of German bureaucracy, so I didn't have a place of my own anymore. I had to stay with my parents. I hadn't stayed with them since I was seventeen years old, and I was quite nervous. We have very different perspectives on life. They like structure and predictability; I crave excitement and the exploration of the unknown. It's difficult for me to imagine living a sedentary life like the one they've opted for. The thought of slaving away at some soul-sapping job just to pay a mortgage makes me feel empty inside. I think there's too much world to see and too many interesting people to meet to waste time thinking about bank balances and retirement accounts. We'll probably never see eye to eye on this issue.

My garden house in Berlin, Germany

5

HELLO, DEUTSCHLAND

I landed in Germany after a twelve-hour flight. The five-hour time difference coupled with the pain medication in my system made me feel like I had a hangover. I was woozy and exhausted as I walked through the jetway and stepped onto German soil. It felt strange hearing people speak in my mother tongue while I made my way through the airport. Having lived in the US for the past twelve years, my ears were no longer accustomed to hearing so much German.

My father met me outside of the baggage claim terminal. I hadn't seen him for quite some time, and I was shocked by how old he looked. His kyphosis—the forward bend in his back—was almost as bad as my kyphosis, which had developed after two separate serious accidents. He'd worked as an electrician for most of his life, and he and my mother ran a restaurant on the weekends. He spent his weeks working for a corporation and his weekends working at our family restaurant, which probably accounted for the bow in his back. The etches on his face were also deeper now, and he had much more gray in his hair. I wondered if he was thinking the same thing about me. Was he looking at my sun-aged face and asking himself where his little girl had gone? I know I often catch myself wondering who that nearly middle-aged woman is staring back at me in the mirror.

My father shook my hand and gave me a formal hug. I don't remember if he even looked at my prosthetic leg, but he certainly didn't say anything about it. In fact, he didn't say much of anything.

From the airport, we drove to my parents' home. The drive was about an hour, and we used the time to catch up on everything that was happening in my parents' lives. But eventually there was a lull in the conversation, and I stared out the window at the trees that line the serpentine highway that leads to their house. That highway dredged up a lot of old memories, including the horrific bicycle accident that nearly cost me my life back in 1989.

When I was still a teenager living at home, I was a triathlete. As part of my daily training workout, I ran or biked fifteen miles through the rolling hills near Stuttgart, where the world-famous Mercedes-Benz production plant is located. I'd had a nasty fight with my mother on the day of the accident. Anytime I argued with my mother, I used exercise to flee the negativity and to sweat out my irritation. I stormed out of my parents' house and jumped on the road bicycle I'd purchased with the money I'd earned from holiday work at a wood factory and from work at my parents' restaurant. I was so proud of my new bicycle after I painted it bright neon green, a really popular color back in the '80s.

I got on the highway and started pushing myself up a steep hill. All the anger and frustration were replaced by adrenaline, especially when I started the descent down that winding highway. I'd biked that stretch of the road many times on other practice runs, and I knew exactly where I had to slow down so as not to lose control. But on that day, I didn't want to slow down. I cranked even harder on my pedals to release all the anger and frustration that had built up during my fight with my mother. I wasn't much concerned about the consequences. And then…well, I don't remember what happened then. Everything I know about the accident came from an eyewitness who saw the wreck.

According to the motorcyclist who watched me go down, I was traveling much too fast for such a sharp turn, and I crashed, tumbled, and slid into the side of a mountain. He found an emergency phone on the side of the highway and contacted 112, Germany's version of 911. When the paramedics arrived, he told them that after the accident, I got up and started walking around, cursing myself for destroying my newly painted bicycle. The front tire was completely bent, and the frame was damaged beyond repair. Apparently, I was far more concerned about the shape of the bicycle than I was about the state of my body.

I didn't become fully aware of my surroundings until I was on a stretcher in an ambulance. I had excruciating pain in my back and numbness in my thumbs, the first sign of paralysis. The road that the ambulance took to the hospital was in very poor condition. There were potholes everywhere, and each time we hit one, tears rolled down my cheeks. To that point in my life, that was the worst pain I'd ever experienced. I couldn't think straight, but I was aware enough to know that the numbness in my thumbs could be a serious problem.

After I arrived at the hospital in a town in Southern Germany, someone contacted my parents. My mother talked to a doctor and made sure they sent me to a hospital that specialized in spinal injuries. The argument I had with her sparked the emotional explosion that resulted in my accident, but her intervention probably prevented me from becoming paralyzed.

Later, in the hospital in Heidelberg, I learned that I'd fractured thoracic and cervical vertebrae. The doctor who treated me told me that I was lucky the damage hadn't been worse. A little more force here, a bit more torque there, and I might have severed my spinal cord. I could have died on the side of that highway, or I might have ended up as a quadriplegic. He also told me that I was lucky my ambulance ride on that bumpy road hadn't exacerbated the injury. One bad jolt and I could have been done as an extreme athlete before I really even started. I felt like a cat that had just lost the first of its nine lives. (If you're keeping track, the skydiving jump that resulted in a dislocated shoulder was my second lost life, and the fall that cost me my leg below the knee was my third. The fourth was when that nurse gave me a heart patient's medication at that rehab facility in Denver.)

For months I lay in a hospital bed in Heidelberg recuperating with a cervical collar wrapped around my neck and a cast encasing my torso from my pelvis to my chest. I wish I could say that I was a model patient, but I constantly argued with my doctor. It seemed like every day he came into my room to tell me what I wouldn't be able to do any more. I could forget about walking—or even sitting—without pain, he told me. I'd have to give up competing in triathlons. I wouldn't be able to pursue a career as a police officer (at the time, I was thinking about becoming a cop or a chef). I told him that he was wrong about everything. I'd do all the things I loved doing, even if it meant that I had to spend all day and night in a gym rehabbing my back and neck. He didn't know me. He probably hadn't had any patients who were as determined and driven as I was, so he couldn't tell me what my future would look like. I was in charge of shaping the course of my life, and I wasn't going to let him define my parameters.

I eventually got sick of lying in that hospital bed, and I was afraid that if I spent too much time there, I'd have to repeat my final year of high school. So, I asked my doctor if I could be released so I could go back to school. He told me that it would be too painful for me to sit in a desk all day. I said I could take the pain, but he said that it wouldn't be responsible for him to discharge me. I asked again and again, then I begged and pleaded, and he eventually grew tired of my harassment and agreed to let me go on the condition that I took my pain meds every day. I consented, although I wasn't keen to rely on medications to overcome my injury. That was my introduction to opioids, and I was lucky I didn't get hooked on them, as it happens so often with other patients.

*"Challenges are what makes life interesting
and overcoming them is what
makes life meaningful."*
~ Joshua J. Marine

I was motivated to prove my doctor wrong about everything, so when I got out of the hospital, I started going to the gym every day to strengthen my core in the hope that it would help me conquer my sometimes-unendurable pain. Six months after the accident, my cast was finally removed. Now that my neck and back-vertebrae were healed, I decided that it was time to start really pushing my body. I gradually increased the length of my workouts until I was exercising for almost six hours a day, cycling to physical therapy, swimming with my swim team, practicing karate, and lifting weights. And it did wonders for my spine. A year after my crash, I had virtually no pain in my back or my neck. I'd done exactly what I'd set out to do, exactly the opposite of what the physician told me I could do. It's funny how little my relationship to doctors has changed in all those years.

An hour after leaving the airport, we arrived at my parents' home. The house was in the middle of nowhere, and it was surrounded by the lakes my grandfather had turned into a business catering to weekend fishermen who paid by the pound to catch trout, bass, and carp, etc. Not much had changed about the house or the surrounding country. It felt like I'd stepped back in time, back to when I was seventeen and living at home, before I left to attend chef school. It was a strange feeling.

The house I grew up in

Years before my return, my parents had renovated their attic, turning it into an apartment for my father's mother, who needed significant assistance in her final years. She has since passed away—she was the last of my grandparents—so they arranged for me to stay in that attic apartment while I was visiting. I had to walk up sixty stairs every time I wanted to get to that room. At that point, I was up to about seventy-five percent strength in my good quad, but my amputated leg had only ten percent of its normal strength. I had to use a cane to limp up and down that staircase, but I didn't complain. I hadn't given up on the idea of regaining full strength in my legs, even if my doctors in the US had. Before leaving therapy, I received a $5,000 wheelchair. They told me that the nerve damage caused by my shattered pelvis would prevent me from walking normally again. But I knew better and was looking forward to proving them wrong, so I left that wheelchair in my camper van back in Denver.

I decided not to look at that staircase as an inconvenience; I'd look at it as part of my training regimen. The more I ascended and descended that small mountain of steps, the closer I'd be to the day when I could toss out that walking cane. One of the most valuable lessons I've learned in my years as an athlete is that your perspective on life can strengthen or break you. If you look at a loss as proof that you're not talented enough or strong enough to win, then chances are you'll never keep up with the competition. But if you can put the sting of the loss behind you and look at your failure as a diagnosis of your weaknesses, then you can set about improving, which is how you'll close the gap between you and your competitors. In other words, setbacks can be a burden or a gift. I was choosing to look at the loss of my leg as a gift. I could once again prove to myself and to the rest of the world that you can accomplish almost anything if you're willing to put in the effort and time to better yourself.

I had a hard time falling asleep in the attic that night. Besides being jetlagged, my mind was racing through time, thinking about all I'd experienced since I'd last slept in that house twenty-three years earlier. I'd moved out of my parents' place when I was seventeen to begin my training to become a chef. For as long as I could remember, my parents had owned a restaurant that served traditional Southern German food such as Schnitzel, Kartoffelsalad, Sauerbraten, Sauerkraut, and Königsberger Klopse, a tasty mix of meats in a white sauce with capers. My parents put me to work cleaning dishes when I was a young child; when I was a little older, they entrusted me with the preparation of the salads and the desserts, all made from scratch. I'm sure that's where I got the idea of becoming a chef.

In Germany, we have a dual education system, which means that if you want to become a chef, you have to work in an actual restaurant for three months, then go to school for a month to learn the theoretical aspects of cooking. A student has to switch back and forth between the practical and the theoretical for three years. The restaurant I started working in after I moved from home provided me with a bed in an employee dorm room I had to share with seven other aspiring chefs. At 7:30 sharp every morning, my classmates and I had to start our prep work: skinning potatoes, dicing vegetables, and slicing onions until we had tears in our eyes.

Working as a chef in my own catering business in Berlin, Germany

That first year was torture. I did nothing but mundane grunt work. I begged my bosses to allow me to do something besides skinning potatoes and cutting onions, but they were deaf to my pleas. Actually, that's not strictly true. On the days when I asked them if I could do something interesting, they asked me to wash and detail their cars and to go shopping for their families. I was dying to get out of that restaurant, but my main boss was the board president of the culinary arts and economics academy. I was afraid that if I burned my bridge with him, I might hurt my chances of becoming a full-time chef. But eventually I decided that I couldn't deal with the boredom anymore, so I found a new restaurant in need of a culinary student. It was a fine dining restaurant with a one-star Michelin rating. Just to give you some perspective, in Germany we currently have a total of ten restaurants with three stars—that's the highest rating—thirty-nine restaurants with two stars, and 215 restaurants with one star. So, landing a spot at even a one-star restaurant was a pretty big deal for a student.

I was much happier at the second restaurant. Besides a jump in my monthly salary from $220 to $350, I was also no longer one of six student trainees. Now I was the only student at my restaurant, which meant that I got a lot more one-on-one time in the kitchen with experienced Chefs. And we made everything from scratch— bread, pasta, pastries, cakes, ice cream—so I learned a lot about every step of meal preparation. There were times when I was surprised by how much responsibility they gave me. There was one day in particular that was especially memorable. My new boss sent me down to the restaurant's basement with a ladder and a razor-sharp knife. I had no idea what he had in mind for me, and I was shocked when I took the elevator down and found a deer hanging from the ceiling.

He looked at me and said, "That'll keep you busy for a while." He told me that I had to remove the hide, quarter the carcass, and cut the meat from the bones.

"Awesome!" I said, beaming.

That was right up my alley. As a kid I'd raised rabbits, and my grandfather taught me how to butcher them. I'd also caught trout in his fishing lakes, and at an early age, I gutted them, so my family could serve them at our restaurant. Sometimes a trout was so fresh that I could still see the heart pumping while I gutted it before my father tossed it into the frying pan; sometimes the fish even jumped out of the pan because the nerves in its body were still twitching. By the way, if you've ever seen a chicken butchered, you'll know what people mean when they talk about someone running around like a chicken with its head cut off. The first time I watched my grandfather use an axe to chop off the head of a rooster, the cock flew off the butcher block and ran circles around the yard, blood squirting from its neck for nearly a minute. It was somewhat traumatizing the first time I saw it, but eventually I got used to the sight.

I wish I could say that my experiences at the second restaurant were all positive, but there were definitely some drawbacks. One of the biggest downsides of transferring before the end of my semester was that my final grade sank to rock bottom because my old boss disapproved of my move and punished me. My new boss also had some anger management issues. When the restaurant was really busy, it was common to see dishes and knives flying through the air. On one occasion, he even tried to slap me in the face because I couldn't find an herb fast enough in the walk-in refrigerator. He might have hit me if my martial arts training hadn't kicked in. I blocked the maneuver easily, and he looked quite embarrassed.

While I was training to be a chef, I worked split shifts. I had a morning and an evening shift, and I spent most of the time between those two shifts in the gym, maintaining the muscle strength I needed to prevent my back pain from flaring up. The gym was quite far from my workplace, so part of my daily exercise routine included riding my bicycle several miles to and from the gym. I spent hours and hours in there, lifting weights and training on a heavy bag. And I was always hungry to try something new, to find some interesting way to test my mental limits and to push my body. I remember that there was a really good-looking Kick-boxing coach who trained a bunch of testosterone-filled young guys. One day I worked up the courage to ask the coach if I could join them. He looked at his assistant trainer and started laughing.

"I don't think so," he said, smiling snidely.

"Why not?" I asked.

He didn't even bother replying.

In the weeks that followed, I pestered him over and over again. I asked him so often that it became a running joke among the guys he was training. They thought it was hilarious that a girl was asking to spar with them.

Eventually the head trainer got sick of listening to me beg, and he asked his assistant, "What do you think? Should we give her a shot?"

"Maybe if she gets knocked on her butt a few times, she'll go away and leave you alone," said the assistant trainer.

I was grinning from ear to ear when they handed me ratty head-gear and a pair of old boxing gloves that smelled like a mix of blood and sweat. They didn't have an extra mouth guard, so the trainer told the young guy they'd picked to be my sparring partner not to hit me in the mouth. But I doubt that he would have even if his trainer hadn't warned him. I'm sure they were all thinking that I was some delicate flower that had to be treated with kid gloves.

I'd earned my green belt in karate, and I had some experience with *kumite*—freestyle sparring in a dojo—but this was the first time I'd ever sparred in the boxing ring, and I was quite excited. My opponent was a typical teenage boy who didn't have much respect for anything or anyone he didn't understand, and he thought I'd be a pushover because I was a chick. He was so cocky that he refused to guard his face with his gloves. That sort of underestimation of my abilities always motivated me, especially when I was a teen. When the trainer gave the signal for us to start, I went straight at him with a one-two-three combo: one punch to his arrogant face, another to his liver, and a third straight kick to his gut. I could tell he wanted to cry, having been embarrassed by a girl, but I had no sympathy for him. I kept pounding away. He quickly realized that he had to protect himself; otherwise he would be knocked out. He started fighting back, and we went five or six rounds. By the end of the match, I'd earned the respect of my opponent, the other boxers, and the trainers. And before I left the gym that day, the trainers invited me to come back again. That was the beginning of my amateur kickboxing and professional boxing careers.

⁓

Waking up in the house I'd grown up in was a surreal experience. Eating breakfast and socializing with my parents, showering in my old bathroom, hearing the familiar creaks in the floorboards—all these reminders of what I'd left behind made me feel conflicted. Part of my brain delighted in hearing long-forgotten sounds and smelling memory-triggering scents, but there's also something vaguely upsetting about revisiting a place after nearly a quarter century's absence and discovering that it's more or less the same as it was the day you left, as if it had been preserved in a time capsule. When you leave the nest at the end of childhood, you learn and grow, you have all sorts of experiences that change the way you view the world. Part of you expects that the rest of the world has changed as much as you have, but then you come back to your childhood home and find that not everything has evolved. It feels a little depressing. It's sort of like meeting old friends at a high school reunion and learning that they had been working the same job since graduation.

After breakfast, I decided that I had to get out of the house, so I made an appointment with my parents' doctor, who was going to be taking care of me while I was in Germany. Among other things, she practices acupuncture. I scheduled several sessions to see if it could be an effective tool for helping me manage my pain and my nerve damage. I've heard so many people tout the benefits of acupuncture, but I'm sad to say that it didn't help me at all. Maybe her technique was a little off, or maybe the practice depends entirely on the placebo effect and my brain isn't capable of the blind faith needed for such healing. Whatever the case, I soon decided to take a more conventional route to manage the pain and to recover my strength.

I started going to physical therapy three times a week to give the muscles in my legs a workout. I decided to buy a used bicycle to ride to all of my therapy sessions as part of my treatment. I also joined my old swim team again. Seeing some of the same faces in the pool more than two decades after I'd last seen them was almost as strange as seeing my childhood home. On top of all of that, I started hiking again all over the neighborhood I'd grown up in.

Me and my old swim team in Germany

Around that time, I received an email from my friend Bobby, a guy I'd met in Hawaii while I was couch-surfing and cycling around Maui and the Big Island in 2011. I'd stayed at his house in Hilo on the Big Island. While there, I watched an active lava flow roll into the ocean; I rode my bicycle up Mauna Kea, the tallest mountain in the state; I went scuba diving at night with manta rays; and I took surfing lessons from an old guy who won the Pipeline Masters competition back in the '70s (he had a long scar that ran down his chest from open-heart surgery, and I hoped I wouldn't have to perform CPR at some point during my lesson). I also hitched a ride from a chatty rabbi who invited me to a party after he dropped me off at Bobby's house. For whatever reason, I later googled him on Bobby's computer, and it turned out that he was a child molester. Needless to say, I didn't go to that party.

Me at the top of Mauna Kea in Hawaii

Bobby had written to tell me that he was in Kiel — it's in Northern Germany —where he'd been taking care of his girlfriend in hospice care for the past three months. A couple days later, I drove 500 miles to see him. Hoping to bring a little happiness into his life, I cooked for him his favorite dish—Rouladen, a German specialty—the way I'd made it for him once in Hawaii. I also took him to a discount shop that sold traditional Southern German clothing. We bought old-style Bavarian outfits and wore them around his girlfriend to cheer her up. We all smiled a lot that day, and I think our time together was helpful for all of us.

Me and Bobby in Kiel, Germany

After we parted ways, I decided to take advantage of the opportunity to do something for myself. I was on the Baltic Sea, and I thought it would be fun to go windsurfing. I'd learned how to windsurf in a youth camp in Greece back when I was a teenager, but I hadn't been on a windsurfing board since then. The guy at the surf shop was incredibly nice. He and his coworker jumped into the water with me and helped stabilize the board, so I could climb on and find my balance point. It was really tricky with a prosthetic leg, but eventually I found the sweet spot. I gripped the sail, and off I went with the wind. I was surfing again!

The owner of the surf shop told me that he was so inspired by my determination that he wasn't going to charge me for the ride. He said that he'd never met someone so strong-willed, and we've been Facebook friends ever since then.

Windsurfing in Kiel, Germany

When I got back to my parents' home, I was introduced to a new prosthetist who could make another leg for me. There weren't many amputees in town, and those who had lost a limb were typically older people who suffered from type 2 diabetes or cancer. I quickly learned that he didn't have much experience with athletic amputees. After a month of visits and phone calls, I gave up on the idea of getting a leg from him. He just couldn't design something that was going to address my needs.

Not long after my arrival at Germany, I'd befriended an Austrian amputee on Facebook. He offered to introduce me to his prosthetist. Because my friend was a triathlete, I figured that his prosthetist would be familiar with the needs of athletes. I didn't need another walking leg, but I'd been itching to go skiing in Austria, so I asked this new prosthetist to build me a ski leg. Not only did he agree to make the leg I wanted, but he also asked one of his staff to go skiing with me for a day to make sure the leg worked for me.

Skiing in the Austrian Alps with my new ski leg

I'd already skied on my prosthetic leg back in the US, shortly after I left the hospital. I had a follow-up appointment with my surgeon, and I came to his office wearing my ski clothing. Seeing how I was dressed, he asked me if I intended to go skiing that day. I assured him that I was only wearing the outfit because it was a cold day and it was the warmest thing I owned. But when I left his office, I headed straight up to the ski slopes. I was tired of doctors and physical therapists telling me what I could and couldn't do, so I stopped arguing with them and did what I wanted to do.

It was late May then, about five and a half months after my accident. In Colorado we sometimes still have snow until early June at a ski resort called Arapahoe Basin, which was where I hired an adaptive ski instructor to teach me how to ski on a prosthetic. To my surprise my instructor had even both legs amputated below the knee. That really inspired me. Rather than giving me ski poles to help me balance, he gave outriggers, which are poles with tiny skis attached to the bottom. Stubborn as I am, I tossed them aside after the first run and replaced them with my traditional ski poles. The first couple runs felt like I'd never skied before, which is a weird experience for someone who worked as a ski instructor for years. But after a couple more runs, I found my ski legs, so to speak and it felt natural again.

"Never give up because great things take time."

~ Dhiren Prajapati

Skiing in Austria with my new ski leg felt awesome because I had more stability with the brace attached directly to my quad. The day went so well that I decided to get online and book an early season hotel stay I got an incredible discount! At a beautiful ski resort with a skiing pass included. I skied every day for the next ten days.

When I got back to my parents' house in Germany, I received a phone call from my prosthetist back in the US. He asked me if I'd consider participating in the inaugural Disabled World Cup in St. Moritz, Switzerland. One of the team members had to pull out of the competition, and the American team needed at least seven athletes to participate. He knew I was an adrenaline junkie, and he remembered that I was in Germany for my brother's wedding. He told me they needed me to compete in the skeleton. I'd never even heard of the sport, but I agreed immediately. I know a once-in-a-lifetime opportunity when I hear it.

He put me in touch with one of the team's coaches, and we worked out all the details. After we finished talking, I searched YouTube for skeleton videos. I found a bunch of maniacs racing around an ice track, riding facedown and headfirst on a flat sled. It's similar to the luge in that both sports use the same courses and rely on gravity to gain speed. But luge athletes race feetfirst on their backs, which changes the racing physics. I did a Google search after watching a few videos and discovered that the skeleton was a Winter Olympic sport back in 1928—in St. Moritz, coincidentally—and then again in 1949, but it was discontinued all the way until 2002. Since then, it has been both a men's and a women's event. I also learned that the sport got its name from the skeleton-looking metal sleds that competitors used back in 1892.

I love pushing myself out of my comfort zone, but I wondered if this was a bit too radical even for me. In the end, I decided that I couldn't back out because I'd already committed to traveling to St. Moritz the next day. And the coach promised that I could go skiing every day, and everything I'd need would be provided at no cost to me. That was an incredible deal. I'd help them field a full team, and they'd give me an all-expenses-paid vacation in the beautiful Swiss mountains.

At 4 a.m. the next morning, I left my parents' house with a cup of coffee still in hand, and drove to St. Moritz, about five hours away by car. When I arrived at the youth hostel that served as the base of operations for the athletes, I met the coaches, including Michael, the guy who had contacted my prosthetist. He was also a below the knee amputee, like me. For amputees, introductions usually include questions about lost limbs. I shared my story about my fall, then I asked him about his leg. He told me a harrowing tale about being shot twenty-one times by the police seven years earlier. He said that he "wasn't exactly a model citizen back then," and he'd been gunned down while running from the cops.

"I'm really, really lucky I didn't die that day," he told me. "Not many people survive twenty-one bullet holes. I can't even say how grateful I am for a second chance at life. And I don't intend to waste a minute. Life's too short not to live every moment to the fullest. If you're making excuses, you're selling yourself short."

Besides coaching, he was a motivational speaker who talked to young kids about the importance of making good decisions. I really appreciated his story, and I was quite impressed that he'd turned his life around so completely.

Later that day, Katie, one of the coaches, introduced me to my skeleton sled, a foam-covered board that slides on steel runners. In our first session, she told me that I had nothing to worry about, that all I had to do was relax on the sled and allow it to gain speed on its own. The faster it traveled, the more stable it would become. She made it sound so simple, but some of my new teammates told me that the event was a lot more involved than Katie was suggesting. They told me that they usually walk up and down the course for several days to memorize all the turns before getting on the sled for the first time. But I didn't have several days. The competition was starting the very next day. I'd have exactly one practice run before I jumped into the deep end of a major international competition.

It wasn't just the track that I was unprepared for. I also didn't have the right uniform. Everyone had an aerodynamic race suit, but I only had my ski pants and a winter jacket. I looked foolish compared to the other athletes, but I wasn't all that concerned about what I wore. Except for the helmet. That was the only piece of equipment that was essential in my book.

I watched the bobsled racers' practice runs, then Katie drove us to the mid-track station starting line. On the way there, I chatted in German with one of my teammates, a guy born in Austria who'd also been invited to participate at the last minute. We tried to reassure ourselves, telling each other that it was no big deal. All you had to do was…nothing, right? That's what Coach Katie had said. We just had to lie on the sled and let gravity do its thing. The faster we went, the more stable the sled would become. Piece of cake, right? Right?!

In spite of our encouraging words to each other, I think it was clear that we were both shitting our pants before the first run. We watched our five other teammates go first so we could figure out exactly what we were supposed to do. We were all amputees who had lost a leg below the knee, so the starting technique was the same for everyone. You had to place your stump on the sled without your prosthetic leg and push off with your good foot. When you got enough speed, you jumped onto the sled, grabbed the handles on top, and tried to relax.

My heart was thumping in my chest like a rabbit when my turn came. I took several deep breaths to calm myself, then I pushed off with all the strength I had in my good leg. I jumped on the sled, and almost immediately it started turning. I hit the banners on both the left and the right side of the track several times. I was grateful that one of my teammates had given me some athletic armor to protect my shoulders and my arms because I'm certain that I would have been horribly bruised otherwise. Eventually I gained sufficient speed, and I took Katie's advice about relaxing. Unlike skeleton courses in the US, the mid-track station in St. Moritz didn't require active steering. Katie had been right. All I had to do was let the course take my sled where it wanted me to go.

Approaching the first curve, I heard the commentators say in *German, "Niki Rellon das ist ihr erster Lauf und in der ersten Kurve hat sie schon eine Geschwindigkeit von 60 Kilometer pro Stunde."* (Niki Rellon, this is her first run, and on the first curve she already has a speed of 37 miles per hour.)

Me in my first skeleton competition in St. Moritz, Switzerland

By the third curve, I'd gained even more speed, and I was traveling almost 47 miles per hours. I tried to lift my head, but the g-force pushing down on my body prevented me from moving. It felt like I was glued to the sled. Everything seemed to be going perfectly, until it suddenly wasn't. Big chunks of track ice hit my shin and the mask of my helmet. I thought I was going to crash, but the ice chunks weren't big enough to stop my momentum. Approaching the last turn, I was traveling almost 56 miles per hour. And after a few more seconds of mind-blowing speed, I crossed the finish line. The entire run had lasted less than three minutes, but it felt more like three hours. It wasn't until after I climbed off the sled that I could really appreciate how much fun I'd just had. I'd been terrified before that first run, but now I was excited for my next trip down the track. I loved this sport!

When I saw Katie, she was incredibly enthusiastic. "Well done!" she yelled, pumping a fist over her head. "Are you ready for tomorrow? The World Cup! Woohoo!"

I threw both of my arms into the air. "I'm born ready!" I replied.

Back at the youth hostel, my teammates and I had drinks with some of the athletes from Great Britain to celebrate our successful practice runs. One of the guys, Charlie, invited me to take a couple shots with him. I obviously had a couple too many because I forgot to set my alarm before I went to sleep, and I woke up the next morning in a panic when I realized what time it was.

Relaxing after my first skeleton practice run

I jumped out of bed, forgetting that I had only one leg. I face planted myself on the floor. Coach Katie knocked on my door moments later.

"You OK?" she asked. "I heard a noise."

"I'm fine. I'll be ready in five," I called back.

There were a few camera crews at the track that morning, and they interviewed some of my teammates. There were also a fair number of spectators. This wasn't exactly the Olympics, but it was still a big deal. I felt a little jittery before my run, a lot like the way I felt before a big fight back in my boxing days. But I was mostly just thrilled to be competing again, a little over six months after I'd nearly fallen to my death. In those final moments before I jumped on my sled at the starting line, I thought back to the bleak days I'd spent in my hospital bed after my surgeries. Never in a million years could I have imagined myself in this situation six months later.

I guess you could say that I had a good run. I wish I could say the same for Charlie, the poor guy who invited me to drink shots with him the previous night, but he didn't place. He finished just behind me, the last medal winner.

My medal after my first skeleton competition in St. Moritz, Switzerland

6

GOODBYE, DEUTSCHLAND

I spent nearly six months in Germany before I was finally able to walk without a cane. I'd been working my butt off in physical therapy. I credit the leg press machine for helping me gain back much of the strength I needed to walk unassisted. But I was still far from 100% strength. In fact, I wasn't even at half strength at that point. The leg press machine I used allowed me to figure out how much strength I'd gained. After establishing a baseline by pushing the press platform with my good leg, I switched over to my prosthetic leg. My left leg was only 40% as strong as my right leg. I was getting there, but I still had a long way to go.

As much as I enjoyed marking the progress I was making toward a full recovery, I was sick of my daily routine: going to the gym, riding my bicycle forty miles a day, swimming with my old team on Mondays, and attending physical therapy three times a week. I was getting itchy feet again. I was also getting depressed, not because I'd lost my leg but because I was living with my parents again. I'd been stuck in their house for the last six months, and I know I'm not alone when I say that it's incredibly challenging to live with your parents again after having traveled the world and been independent for so many years. I just couldn't do it anymore.

Part of the problem was that my parents were constantly trying to convince me to go back to school, so I could start a new profession, some kind of office job that didn't require much physical activity. I thought they were crazy for thinking I could sit behind a desk all day long. They obviously didn't realize how excruciating it was for me to sit for long stretches. In fact, my father didn't realized that I was in pain. I didn't really talk much about my pain, but I assumed that he would know that, if someone cut off your leg six months prior, and you had countless other injuries, you would be suffering physically. I was wrong, though. My father saw my pain meds one day and asked if I was in pain. My mother obviously had a better understanding of my condition because before I could reply, she answered the question for me, that she has pain as well.

I just don't understand how they could think I could sit in a class-room all day when I couldn't even sleep at night because of severe nerve pain. And how could I stay motivated to study something I had no interest in learning!? I was frustrated that they seemed to know so little about what makes me tick.

"When I hear someone sigh, life is hard, I'm always tempted to ask, compared to what?"
~ Sydney Harris

As if to shake me out of my doldrums, life gave me another challenge around this time. When I was in training as a triathlete back when I was a teen, I never rode my bike on bicycle paths, but now that I had a prosthetic leg, I felt like I needed to work my way up to riding with the cars again. One day I was riding on a bicycle path through a small village, and I came to a side road. I had the right of way, but a car pulled out in front of me. I T-boned it and flew over the hood, landing on my back on the opposite side.

I started yelling at the motorist, who'd clearly been in the wrong: *"Du arschloch, hast du nicht mehr alle tassen im Schrank?!"*

I was terrified that I'd reinjured something I'd broken during my fall in Utah. The thought of another long hospital stay made my hands shake. I checked myself for broken bones, probing and squeezing my body in search of pain. I didn't find any obvious injuries, but my adrenalin was pumping, so I might not have noticed immediately if I'd broken anything.

An ambulance soon arrived, and the paramedics loaded me onto a gurney and took me to the local hospital. I was diagnosed with a concussion, and I had to stay overnight for observation. I hated sleeping in a hospital again, but all things considered, I think I got lucky. The accident could have been much, much worse.

When I read the police report a couple days later, I was shocked to see that the officer who arrived on the scene assigned some of the blame to me. The report stated that "Miss Rellon was cycling too fast," and the driver who pulled out in front of me wasn't held completely liable for the accident. I think the police officer who wrote the report was full of baloney, but I also think it's ironic that a woman who was lying in bed with a shattered body and an amputated leg ten months earlier could be held partially responsible for an accident due to excessive speed on a bicycle.

German newspaper report about my accident

Intersection where I was hit by a car

Because of the accident, I was approved for rehab training in Bavaria, the most southern state in Germany.

At that time my nerve pain was getting out of control, and they extended my stay for two more weeks, and my doctor prescribed a higher dosage of opioids, to keep the nerve pain under control.

After the bicycle crash, my insurance paid for a new walking leg. The rehab center had a prosthetist on site, and I'm happy to say that he knew exactly what he was doing.

My fortieth birthday was quickly approaching, but it didn't look like anyone from my family was planning to travel to the rehab center to visit me. The thought of spending such a significant milestone alone depressed me, but I lucked into a fun night. I met a woman named Kerstin, who was in rehab for a dislocated disc in her back. She told me that she had tickets for a Chippendales show on the night of my birthday, and she invited me to come with her. Woohoo! I spent my big 4-0 ogling ripped dancers who all looked like they belonged in the movies. The group photo after the show was the cherry on top of a spectacular night.

Hanging out with the Chippendales on my fortieth birthday

Toward the end of my allotted eight weeks in rehab, I noticed that I was making a lot of excuses not to exercise. If it rained, I told myself that I shouldn't ride my bicycle because the roads would be slick, and I might fall, but if I didn't ride my bicycle, I couldn't get to the gym to lift weights or to the pool to swim laps. If my nerve pain was especially bad, I'd take an extra pain pill, and suddenly rest and comfort food seemed more important than exercise. The more I slacked off, the more weight I gained and the less happy I felt. I started searching the internet for an escape from my boring daily routine. I wanted to find something that would challenge my body and my mind and would help me close the strength gap between my two legs. I needed to do something that would eliminate the possibility of excuses, something like working on the Bounty as a deckhand or riding my bicycle across the country.

After days of searching, I stumbled across some articles about people who'd hiked the Appalachian Trail (AT). Back in 2006, I'd hiked the 2,600-mile Pacific Crest Trail (PCT) over the course of six months, and I'd learned a lot about the AT from the hikers I'd encountered on the PCT. I decided back then that I'd hike the AT one day, but I wasn't sure if now was the right time. Hiking the 2,200-path from Georgia to Maine was difficult enough for people with two legs. How would someone with a prosthetic leg cope with the challenges thrown at the hiker on a daily basis?

Me at the ending point of the PCT in Manning Park
in British Columbia, Canada, in 2006

As if in answer to my question, I came across an online article about a guy named Scott Rogers, who, in 2004, became the first above-the-knee amputee to hike the whole Appalachian Trail, from Georgia to Maine. The thirty-five-year-old guy had lost his leg in 1998 when he accidentally shot himself. Nicknamed "One Leg" by other AT hikers, Rogers walked on a sophisticated prosthetic that used hydraulics and microprocessors to help him maintain his balance, although he occasionally had to use crutches when the pain in his stump became unbearable. His accomplishment was a source of inspiration for both able-bodied and disabled hikers.

I finished the article and looked him up on Facebook. He accepted my friend request, and eventually we chatted over Skype. I was quite impressed with what he'd done, especially because he had an above-the-knee prosthetic leg, which requires batteries to power the knee joint. After talking with him for more than an hour, I felt confident that I'd found my next challenge. His prosthetic required batteries that had to be recharged every other day. If he could hike the AT, then I could do it on a below-the-knee prosthetic. It would still be ridiculously hard, but it wouldn't be quite as difficult as what he'd done.

This was it! This was my escape plan! Walking the AT would help me to regain the strength I'd had before my accident. When you're on the trail, you can't make excuses. It's impossible to carry all the calories you need for the entire hike, so you have to mail food to yourself and pick it up at post offices at strategic locations along the trail, which means that you can't take days off and sit around being lazy. You have a certain amount of food for a certain number of days, and if you run out before you pick up your next food box, then you either starve or you hope that you can find someone to mooch off until you can make it to your next box, but nobody wants to be a trail mooch. So, you push on. You get up every morning and tend to the blisters on your feet or your hips or your shoulders or all of the above, then you walk and walk and walk. And after collapsing into sleep at the end of each day, you wake up the next morning and start all over again. You do the same thing day after day after day until you finish, or you quit and go home.

Thrilled with the prospect of this new test of my endurance and my will, I sat down and started planning. From what I remembered of hiking the PCT, it's important to remove every excess ounce from your pack, so I began hunting for the lightweight gear I'd have to carry on my back every day for however many months it would take me to hike from Georgia to Maine. And it was essential for me, with my still-mending body, to find gear that would put as little strain as possible on my back and on my stump. The sleeping bag I'd used on the PCT was still in fabulous shape, so I could check that item off my list. I could also reuse the Pepsi-can stove that a friend had helped me make back in 2006.

Trail-Angel helping me craft a Pepsi-can stove

I loved that stove. It was made from parts of two aluminum cans, and it weighed less than an ounce altogether. It was also so sturdy that it lasted my entire six-month hike of the PCT, and I never once had a problem with it. I boiled countless pots of water for soups and for coffee, which kept me warm on many cold nights and mornings. More than that, it literally saved my life one day while I was hiking up from lower elevation to the point where rain became snow. Eventually the snowfall became so heavy that I couldn't see the trail, so I pitched my tent. When I pulled out from my dry bag the sleeping bag, I discovered that my bag was soaking wet. Shivering inside my tent, I used my Pepsi-can stove to boil water, which I put into my drinking bladder to keep me warm. I repeated that process all night until sunrise. The next morning, I hiked twenty miles to a trailhead, then I found a motel for hikers and took a hot shower for what seemed like hours.

After doing some online digging, I found an internet company that makes cuben fiber, super ultra-lightweight tents and backpacks. I ordered one of each and had them delivered to the home of a friend I'd met in Georgia while I was cycling across the country. Diane and I had talked on Skype about my plans to hike the AT. She told me that she loved the idea of following me on Facebook while I walked to recover my strength, especially since she'd recently finished walking the Camino de Santiago, a series of pilgrimage paths that runs across Europe and joins together at the tomb of St. James in Santiago de Compostela, a UNESCO World Heritage Site in the northwest of Spain. I thought her experiences might somehow help me with my hike, so I asked her a few questions.

"Which route did you hike?"

"The Camino Frances. It's the most popular one. It runs something like 500 miles from St. Jean-Pied-du-Port in France to Santiago. It was great, but it got really crowded during mid-summer."

"Did you enjoy it?"

"Yeah, except half the people on the trail talked about God all day. But it is a pilgrimage, so I guess I shouldn't have been surprised."

"What did the other half talk about?"

"Usually about how many miles they'd hiked that day and how fast they were moving. That got on my nerves, so I jumped on a train and skipped some sections."

"What was your favorite part?"

"I loved the public fountains in some of the small villages. Instead of water, they dispensed wine. It seemed like everyone was drinking wine with every meal."

She finished telling me about her adventure, then we talked about the nuts and bolts of mine. Besides letting me have my new backpack and tent delivered to her house, she asked if she could join me at the kick-off party at Springer Mountain, where I'd officially start hiking the AT. She also suggested that I hang out with her for a few days before starting the hike, so we could catch up and have some fun together. We were both excited. It's funny how much your perspective can change when you start working toward a goal.

Cuben fiber tent and backpack

Soon after my talk with Diane, I booked a plane ticket back to Denver. My top priority was meeting with my prosthetist to make sure I had the best leg for hiking 2,200 miles. I didn't know if I could walk the whole distance, but I knew I wanted to try. I wanted to recover my strength. I wanted to become the person I'd been before my accident, or at least as close to that as possible. To do all that, I needed whatever help I could get from my prosthetist.

The night before my departure to Denver, my mother cooked a going-away meal for the whole family, including my brother, his new wife, and their baby daughter. I invited an old friend I'd known since I was a teenager. The meal was great, and I enjoyed that final night with everyone, but I was excited to get back to the US, so I could start this new chapter of my life.

My flight left very early the next morning. I gave a huge hug to the big cat I'd recently adopted. I called him Lutzifer. He was a "secondhand cat" from Craigslist, and I got him as a replacement for the cat that had died just before my arrival. He comforted me for eight months, following me wherever I went. At one point, I tried to put him on a leash to see if I could get him to hike with me, but he dropped all of his twelve pounds of black, furry flab to the ground and refused to budge. I also said goodbye to my mother, who got up extra early to see me off. She promised to take care of my cat, and we also shared a hug.

Lutzifer, my secondhand cat from Craigslist

My father drove me to the airport along that same serpentine highway I'd crashed on when I was sixteen. After we said our goodbyes, I headed to the check-in gate. I was expecting to pass right through, but I ran into a problem. When I arrived in Germany eight months earlier, I'd given my German passport to the customs agent, but this time I handed my American passport to the ticket agent. She thought I'd illegally overstayed my ninety-day visa, which would have meant tremendous difficulties to reenter Germany ever again. But I quickly explained the situation as I unpacked my luggage to find my German passport. After I handed it over, the agent checked everything out, and I was finally sent on my way.

Now that I'm an amputee, I always take advantage of the wheelchair assistance offered by most airports, so I don't have to stand in line. But that doesn't mean I get through security any faster than everyone else. The titanium screws in my pelvis and my stump always set off metal detectors, and I have to wait for a specially trained security agent to pat me down and check me with a handheld wand. It's not at all convenient, but after everything I've endured, it's nothing I can't handle.

Liner with the pin-lock system

Getting wheelchair assistance at the airport

Staring out over Germany as the plane took off for the US, I breathed a sigh of relief. It felt like a burden was being lifted from my shoulders. It wasn't just that I was excited to be on my own again. I also was really looking forward to being around Americans. In Germany, lots of people gawked at my prosthetic leg like I was a freak, and they refused to look me in the eye when I caught them staring. I even got a nasty look from a German nun once, probably because she thought the skull on my socket was something demonic. But in the US, people usually see my leg and give me a compliment about my toughness or about the cool Grateful Dead image on the socket. Americans almost never make me feel inferior because of my injury. They make me feel welcome, and I was happy to be on my way home.

7

OLD FRIENDS, NEW FRIENDS

Before I left Germany, my prosthetist had made arrangements for me to stay at the same charity hotel I'd lived in for a month after being discharged by the Medical Center the year before. The time I spent in the hotel the previous year was one of the lowest points of my life, so I wasn't exactly thrilled to be back. Being there brought back a lot of miserable memories, but I reminded myself that it was only temporary. I'd soon be starting on a journey that only one person had ever taken.

Not long after I arrived at the hotel, I contacted the snowboarding coach I'd met the first time I'd skied on my prosthetic leg. He'd spotted me and suggested that I join the adaptive snowboarding team. There was still snow on the mountains, so he invited me to come up for a day of snowboarding and skiing. I drove my old camper van to Copper Mountain, a ski resort in Summit County, where the coach gave me a complimentary ski pass. It was a gorgeous, cloudless day, the perfect conditions for some fun on the snow. We ripped that mountain together for a couple hours, then I drove back to my hotel room.

That same day, I received a message over Facebook from someone I knew by reputation but had never met. His name is John, and he's a rock-climbing legend, not to mention the author of more than forty books and the original screenwriter of *Cliffhanger*, the 1993 movie starring Sylvester Stallone. He was also one of the founding members of a group of elite climbers called the Stonemasters, who launched the extreme sports movement in the '70s.

Back in 2012, John was seriously injured when he fell from a wall in a climbing gym in Los Angeles. His bowline came untied, and he suffered a compound fracture of his left leg and ankle. He befriended me on Facebook because he was considering an amputation, and he was curious about my recovery. He said he was inspired by my story, and he asked if I was interested in getting sponsorship from Adidas. What?! Sponsorship from Adidas?! That's my all-time favorite brand for athletic gear, and not just because it's a German company. They make incredible clothing, shoes, protective gear—incredible everything. It sounded too good to be true.

John told me that Adidas was part of a big climbing event that took place at the end of 2014. Tommy Caldwell and Kevin Jorgeson, two legends in the climbing world, free climbed the Dawn Wall route on El Capitan, a sheer cliff face in Yosemite National Park in California. After years of preparation, the pair free climbed what most climbers consider the hardest route in the world. For those who aren't familiar with climbing lingo, a "free climb" is a climb without any assistance, whereas "aid climbing" involves using devices that help a climber make upward progress. Free climbers only use their hands and feet to move up the mountain, but they are attached to a rope to prevent death in case of a fall. Free climbers are monstrously strong athletes with ice water running through their veins, but even those guys aren't crazy enough to climb the Dawn Wall without a harness and a rope.

This wasn't just a major event in the world of climbing; this was a major event period. Camera crews from all over the world had filmed the two climbers as they made their way up the granite face of that mountain over nineteen days. It was such a big deal that President Obama called to congratulate Tommy and Kevin after they reached the top. Those guys are rock-climbing royalty, and their names are known by people all over the world.

John thought that Adidas might be interested in shooting a documentary of firsts: the first free climbers of Dawn Wall and the first woman amputee to thru-hike the Appalachian Trail. Was I interested? Hell, yeah, I was interested!

Days after I talked to John, a woman named Dorothy from the Los Angeles headquarters of Adidas emailed me a plane ticket. I was taking an all-expenses-paid vacation to sunny California to visit the offices of my favorite clothing company. And it had all been arranged by a rock-climbing god who'd reached out to me. It felt like I was dreaming.

Before I left for Los Angeles, I decided that I needed to take care of some unpleasant business I'd been putting off. Before amputating my leg, Dr.H agreed that he'd save it for me, so I could dispose of it when I was ready. Well now I was ready. I intended to pick up the leg from the hospital and have a Burning Man-like bonfire to cremate it (for those who don't know, the Burning Man Festival is a massive annual party held in Black Rock Desert in Northern Nevada, and the experiment in radical self-expression always ends with a huge ritual bonfire). I wanted to have a burning-leg party in someone's backyard in Denver. I thought it would be an incredible sendoff for a body part that had been near and dear to me for almost forty years.

Just a couple days before I was scheduled to leave for Los Angeles, I visited my prosthetist's office for some fine tuning of my leg. While I was in the waiting room, I called the pathology department.

"Hi. My name's Niki Rellon," I told the woman who answered the phone. "I was a patient back in the beginning of 2014. My left leg was amputated and put in a freezer for storage. Dr. H. was my surgeon. I'm calling to arrange pick-up."

She put me on hold for a few minutes, then she returned with the news. "We have your leg, but it's been in a cooler."

"You mean a freezer?" I asked. I assumed that she was talking about something that got cold enough to freeze tissue. I thought that maybe they had different terminology for a freezer in a hospital.

"No, not a freezer. A cooler. Like a refrigerator."

"What do you mean?!" I snapped. I couldn't believe what I was hearing, and I was suddenly seeing red. "It's been fourteen goddamn months! It was supposed to be in a freezer."

"I'm sorry," she said, not sounding at all apologetic. "There must have been a mix-up."

"It's going to be rotten now. There's not going to be anything left but bones and ligaments."

"And it's going to stink to high heaven," she added.

"Great!"

"I'm sorry."

"Well, I want my leg back!" I barked. "When can I pick it up?"

"You'll have to arrange for a funeral. It's considered hazardous material now, and we can't just let you walk out of the hospital with it."

"So, I'm supposed to pay a thousand bucks or whatever for a ridiculous funeral? Do you know how dumb that sounds? Funerals are for dead people, not for rotten legs. Am I supposed to have a head-stone or something that says, 'Here lies Niki Rellon's left leg'?"

"I'm really sorry, Ms. Rellon, but there's nothing I can do about it. This isn't just a hospital policy. This is state law."

"Dammit!" I hissed between clenched teeth. "This isn't right."

"I'm so sorry."

"Well I'd like to see it one more time at least. I never got to say goodbye. And I'd like to take some photos if possible."

She put me on hold again, and she went off in search of a supervisor who would know more about the situation. When she came back on the line, she gave me more heartbreaking news. "I'm so sorry, but we're not legally allowed to show it to you either. It's a health hazard."

"Fine," I growled, and I hung up on her.

I looked up and saw my prosthetist's assistant striding over to me. "You can't have conversations like that in this office!" he barked. The jugular vein in his neck bulged and throbbed, and his face was blood red.

I looked around the room. There wasn't anyone else there but me. "What's the big deal? No one's here."

"This isn't the place for a conversation like that."

I raised my hands in surrender. "Fine. It won't happen again."

Needless to say, I was irate that my plans had all been shot to hell, but I didn't want to burn any bridges with my prosthetist. I relied on his support in more ways than one. After picking up a new leg from him, I hurried out of his office, so I could blow off some steam.

I arrived at LAX a couple days later. Dorothy, the woman who'd mailed me the ticket, picked me up and took me to a hotel. After I checked in, a butler showed me to my room. I was in awe of the place. It reminded me of the fancy hotels in Berlin I'd worked in as a chef in my catering business.

I took a quick shower and a nap, then Adidas sent a car to the hotel to pick me up for dinner. Dorothy, John, and John's editor were waiting for me inside the car. I'd been hearing about John's exploits for years, so it was quite an honor for me to meet him. He bent over backwards to make me feel comfortable. He asked about my favorite food. I told him that I love clean, healthy food like sushi, so we drove to an awesome sushi restaurant in downtown LA. While we ate, he shared all sorts of interesting stories about his life, and I'm grateful that I got to meet him in person.

The next morning, another car brought me to the Adidas head-quarters, where I found a factory full of incredible athletic gear. Dorothy told me that she'd ordered a bunch of clothes and shoes for me, and she wanted me to try everything on to see if it all fit. I felt like I'd died and gone to Adidas heaven. Jackets, shirts, pants, shoes— it was incredible! I love the smell of new clothing, especially Adidas clothing. When John arrived, and saw my saucer eyes, he could tell I was overwhelmed. He told me not to be shy, insisting that I could have everything I wanted from a rack that was chock-full of gear. I counted at least eight pairs of hiking pants, several incredibly expensive jackets, sweatshirts, T-shirts, etc. I'm not sure if Dorothy really meant for me to take all the clothing on the rack, so I held back.

Dorothy, John, John's editor, and the Adidas crew at a sushi restaurant in LA

John's editor then showed up with a GoPro camera, telling me that I should use it while I was hiking the AT for the documentary that John had proposed that Adidas shoot. He also interviewed me, which marked the official beginning of the documentary. As I answered his questions, my mind stepped out of my body for a moment, and I realized how strange this all was. Fourteen months earlier, I thought my life was more or less over. But here I was sitting in an Adidas factory being interviewed for a documentary about firsts. It was an unbelievable turn of events.

I spent two days in LA, then John invited me to drive down to San Diego with him and with another rock climber who was famous in the climbing world. We all participated in an indoor rock climbing event, and John and I spent a lot of time talking about how I should film myself for the documentary. When we returned to LA, Dorothy arranged a flight for me to Jacksonville, Florida. I left LA equipped with two bloated Adidas bags filled with incredible gear and with new relationships with some impressive people.

My very good friend Diane, the one who'd recently hiked the Camino de Santiago, picked me up from the airport in Jacksonville. We drove about an hour to her place in Brunswick, Georgia. The next morning, we had breakfast at her favorite joint. While we ate, we reminisced about some of the adventures that we'd shared a decade earlier.

"Do you remember when we met in 2003, when I was bicycling from Key West to New York City?"

"Hell yeah!" she exclaimed. "That was quite some fun we had together."

"Yeah, especially when I made it to New York City on my way to catch a plane back to Germany, and I found you were in New York, so we visited the Metropolitan Museum of Art together."

"Yes, I remember," she said.

"Then, you fell on that stupid set of steps afterwards," I added.

"Yes, indeed! I had to push you with a wheelchair through New York City. But the best memory I have in that time," she said, "was when you used couchsurfing.com to stay with that Indian guy who gave a party."

"Yeah," I responded. "And you brought all your girlfriends to that party too. I think that guy from India was in girl's heaven at that time, with four blondes at his party!"

"I also remember when I drove you to Charleston, South Carolina, to that other couchsurfing.com host," she said. "He picked you up in his red Cadillac."

"Absolutely, I remember him," I replied. "He was a very handsome, good-looking guy. He gave me the prime tour through Charleston in his convertible and afterwards he had tickets for a concert. I think I got laid that evening."

We were laughing as we left that breakfast joint.

In NYC with Diane and her friends at my Couchsurfing host's apartment

Later that day, Diane told me that she was taking me out to dinner. On the drive from her house, she warned me that she'd invited some friends who wanted to know a little about my proposed hike on the AT. I told her that I didn't mind. Any friend of hers was a friend of mine.

I thought it was strange when she parked her car outside a convention center. I guessed that there was a restaurant inside for convention attendees. Just moments after we walked through the front doors, a guy about my age approached me with an outstretched hand.

"You must be Niki," he said.

"That's me," I replied, shaking his hand. "Niki Rellon. Nice to meet you." I guessed that this was one of the friends Diane had told me about.

"I can't wait to hear your talk," he said. "I've read about your fall. It sounded horrible."

"What talk?" I had no idea what he was talking about.

He pointed to a stage set up in front of dozens of chairs. "I think they're ready for you to start whenever you're ready."

My eyes widened, and I turned to Diane for an explanation. She gave a sheepish shrug.

"Don't hate me," she said, smiling hesitantly. "It was just a little spontaneous thing. I thought nobody would show up. I had no idea the turnout would be so good."

"Are you ready to start?" asked the guy who'd introduced himself.

I shook my head at Diane and smiled in disbelief. "We'd better still be going to dinner after this."

"I promise we'll go. And it's on me," she said. "Now get out there and have fun."

So, I did what many people have nightmares about: I walked onto a stage in front of a crowd of people and, with absolutely no preparation, gave a speech. It's a good thing I'm an extrovert who doesn't get stage fright, otherwise I never would have been able to talk about my fall and about my recovery to that point. It also helped that I'd worked as a professional ski instructor for many years. I'd stood in front of big groups of people and lectured about the ins and outs of skiing for hours every day.

The speech and the questions and answers that followed lasted more than an hour. As soon I finished, I hurried off stage and found Diane.

"What were you thinking?!" I asked.

She grinned impishly. "What's the big deal? It went great. Everybody loved you. You even got some laughs."

"You could have at least given me a heads up, so I could prepare," I said. "Can we go to dinner now?"

⌒

Final preparations for my Appalachian Trail hike began the next morning at a grocery store. My experiences on the Pacific Crest Trail had taught me that it's better to rely on a friend who can supply you with sustenance by mailing boxes of food to local post offices along the trail rather than to rely on little gas stations along the way, because you never know what you're going to find in those tiny stores. It's smart to buy at least some of the food you'll need for certain sections of the hike and ask a friend to parcel it out for you.

My supply person on the Pacific Crest Trail was a guy named Tom. I'd met him in Arizona Hot Springs the year before I started hiking the PCT. At the time, I was helping a friend I'd met while I was traveling across the country in 2002. I was cycling on the Pacific Coast Highway, and he was driving in his RV. We met at a picnic stop and started talking about our travels. Jeffrey had decided to take a break from his life to discover America. We stayed in touch online, and we met up again a couple weeks later when I reached San Diego. He really wanted company while he traveled, so he asked me to join him in his RV trip to Florida. He even offered to buy me a brand-new touring bicycle once we arrived. What a guy!

The bicycle I'd brought from Germany was falling apart, so it didn't take any arm-twisting for me to take him up on his offer. Jeffrey kept his word. After three months of touring the country with him in his RV, he bought me a new long-distance bicycle.

I once heard an American say:

"IF YOU GIVE A HORSE TO A COWGIRL,
SHE TAKES OFF."

Jeffrey on the Pacific Coast Highway

I'd only planned on touring on my bicycle for six months, but now that I had a new one, I couldn't resist the call of the road. I cycled to Key West, to New York City, to San Francisco, back down to San Diego again, to Baja California, to La Paz, to Mazatlán (by ferry), and to Mexico City. Then I took a plane to Miami and rode back up to New York City for a second time. From there, I flew back to Germany.

A year later, in 2005, I decided to get a green card, so I could live in the US. I flew from Germany to Nova Scotia, Canada, and from there I cycled to Colorado, where Jeffrey picked me up in his RV (Jeffrey turned out to be an attorney, and years later, in 2011, he helped me fill out the paperwork to become a US citizen). We drove together to New Mexico. There I helped him build his house in a small town called Truth or Consequences. Back in the '50s, the town had been called Hot Springs, but the townsfolk changed the name of their home to win a contest run by a TV show called, you guessed it, *Truth or Consequences*. Like most people, I smiled the first time I heard the name. I think later generations were probably a little embarrassed by the name because I only ever heard them refer to the town as "T or C."

Moments before becoming a US citizen in 2011   Taking the citizenship oath

While I was helping Jeffrey build his house, I met another German woman who was a ski instructor at a resort in Ruidoso, New Mexico. I asked her if she could set me up with an affordable ski pass. She told me that I should just become a ski instructor, so I could get paid to ski all day every day of the season. I told her I'd never worked as a ski instructor, but she said I shouldn't worry. There was a hiring clinic in a couple days. All I had to do was show up on the mountain with my ski gear, and they would teach me everything I needed to know to become a ski instructor.

That day I went to a Salvation Army store to buy some second-hand gear. I found skis from the late '80s, a pair of boots that were two sizes too big, and ski poles. I showed up on the mountain the next day in my ill-fitting, out-of-date gear. I was certain I wasn't going to get the job, but after several runs down the slopes, they offered it to me. I was officially a paid ski instructor. But they told me I'd have to use some of their rental gear until I could get some better stuff for myself. I guess they didn't want me looking like I'd stepped out of a bad '80s skiing movie.

Starting on my first day as an instructor, I woke up every morning at 5:30 and cycled up the mountain from Ruidoso. It was only fourteen miles, but the elevation change was more than 6,000 feet. At the time, I was planning my PCT hike, and I thought that a strenuous ride up a mountain every day would be a great way to whip my body into shape for the 2,600-mile hike from Mexico to Canada. It was also a gorgeous ride, and on at least one occasion, I saw wild mustangs romping around in a field on the mountain. Inspired by my daily ride up to the resort, several other instructors cycled up with me one morning. But that was the one and only time anyone ever rode with me. They all said it was too exhausting to make that trek before strapping on a pair of skis and making runs down the slopes all day. But they respected me for making the daily trip on my bicycle, and from that first morning on, they gave me a standing ovation every time I made it to the top.

When the season ended the next spring, I said goodbye to my new ski instructor friends, and I hopped on my bicycle. I decided to ride from Ruidoso to San Diego, where I'd start hiking the PCT. On my way out there, I stopped by Arizona Hot Springs, which is in a slot canyon that empties into a river downstream from Ringbolt Rapids. This wasn't the first time I'd visited these hot springs. Back when I was riding my bicycle across the country, I'd found it on my map, and I rode more than a hundred miles out of my way to visit the place. I guess you could say that I'm a hot spring junkie. But what's not to love about sitting in 111-degree water in the middle of the desert?

I wouldn't dare leave my fully loaded bicycle unattended on the road, not when it had my tent, my sleeping bag, and everything else

I needed to hike the PCT. So, I decided to carry everything down with me. I pitched my tent on the bottom of the canyon next to the river, where I could almost see Hoover Dam. After I settled in, I climbed up into the springs using a steel ladder that was bolted into the stone wall. I soaked in the hot springs until sunset, then I made my way back to my camp. I was surprised to find another tent pitched directly next to my tent. With so much free space down there, it seemed a little rude for someone to set up camp so close to mine. In the distance, I saw a guy building a campfire not far from a kayak. He was about my age, six feet tall, and good-looking. I approached him and asked him why he'd put his tent so close to mine. He apologized profusely, telling me that he thought that my tent belonged to a buddy he was meeting in the canyon. They'd made plans to meet down there to celebrate his friend's birthday, but they'd come separately. His friend still hadn't shown up, which worried him a little now that it was after dark.

But we soon saw a light on the river. Tom, the guy I'd met, yelled for his friend, Jeff. Eventually Jeff found his way to shore. We helped him set up his camp, and the three of us celebrated Jeff's birthday German style: Jägermeister shots all around. I'd expected a quiet night by myself, but I ended up partying with two great guys instead. Unexpected moments like these are one of my favorite parts of traveling. You never know when you're going to bump into a new friend around the next bend.

The next morning, Jeff didn't feel well. I think he had a hangover. I'd planned on spending some more time in the hot springs that morning, but Jeff offered to let me use his kayak while he recovered in his tent. He recommended that Tom and I take a trip down the river to see if we could find another hot spring that was supposed to be even more magnificent than the one I'd soaked in on the previous day.

Arizona Hot Springs ladder   Celebrating Jeff's birthday
                                          with Tom

So, Tom and I climbed into separate kayaks, and together we headed toward Hoover Dam. The morning was a little chilly, but I quickly warmed up as I paddled down the river. There wasn't much greenery to see along the way, but the red-brown cliffs that surrounded us were beautiful for their starkness. We made our way to the base of the dam, where we climbed out of the kayaks and hiked up to a sauna cave that was discovered by the construction workers who built the dam back in the 1930s. The workers began drilling a tunnel through the cave, but they had to abandon the project when they found pressurized water that was about 122 degrees. It's now a popular destination for hikers and hot springs lovers like me.

Although there isn't much foliage in the area, there is a grove of tamarisk bushes right outside the entrance of the cave. Once you pass the grove and climb up into the cave, you wade into knee-deep water. The tunnel extends about a hundred feet into the mountain. It's hot and humid and very dark. We didn't have a flashlight, but we managed to find the end of the tunnel, and we had a nice soak before moving on.

Kayaking toward Hoover Dam

We climbed back into our kayaks and continued paddling down the river to find the Goldstrike Hot Springs, which is even closer to the dam than the sauna cave. It wasn't possible to access it from the river, so we docked the kayaks on the shore and hiked to Goldstrike. The hot springs drain into the river, which meant that we just had to follow the warm water upstream. We had to do some technical climbing, but previous hikers had left ropes that we used to find the pool. When we arrived, we looked up and saw that the canyon walls rose straight up from the water. They shielded us from the sun and created pretty little waterfalls. Because no one was there, we had the entire pool to ourselves. We enjoyed a blissful, peaceful day together, and we lost track of time completely. Before we knew it, the sky was dimming. Sunset was right around the corner, and we still had to hike back to our kayaks and paddle down the river against the current to get back to our campsite. It was fairly dark by the time we made it to the kayaks, but we managed on the river just fine.

When we got back to camp, Jeff was obviously worried. "Are you OK? What happened?" he asked.

"Sex happened," Tom said with a smile.

Soaking at Arizona Hot Springs   Goldstrike Hot Springs

When I told Tom that I was on my way to San Diego to hike the PCT, he became very excited. He told me that he lived in Aspen, Colorado, and he had some mountaineering experience. He offered to support me on the trail with food supplies, and he even asked if he could hike part of the trail with me, a section called the John Muir Trail (JMT), which runs through the Sierra Nevada's. The JMT is about 210 miles long, and it rises in elevation approximately 47,000 feet. It passes through alpine and high mountain terrain in Yosemite, Kings Canyon, and Sequoia National Parks. Although the JMT is known by many hikers as America's most famous trail, there usually aren't many people hiking it at any given time. It's rare to run into anyone while on the JMT.

Tom, Jeff, and I stayed a couple days longer, then we packed our gear and prepared to hike out. While Jeff paddled back to his car, Tom and I carried our gear out of the canyon to the spot where Tom had parked. We drove through Death Valley together and visited another remote hot spring. Then we parted ways, and I jumped on my bicycle and headed for the Mexican border near San Diego, where I started hiking the PCT. It would take me almost six months to get to Canada, 2,600 miles away.

On my way to the Mexican border, where I began hiking

At the southern terminus of the PCT

After I finished grocery shopping, I returned to Diane's house and made fifteen resupply boxes for the AT. I packed the last box sometime in the early afternoon. I was thinking about getting on the internet and doing a little research on post offices near the trail when the doorbell rang. Diane opened the door and greeted a man and a woman. Diane was wearing the same hesitant smile she'd worn the night before.

"Oops," she said. "I forgot to tell you that I called our local paper and told them about your hike. Don't hate me."

"Seriously? Again?" I shook my head as she introduced me to the reporter and her cameraman. I couldn't believe that she'd sprung another surprise on me. "Can I at least have a few minutes to get cleaned up for the photos?"

"Hurry," she said.

"Yeah, yeah," I said before excusing myself to freshen up. I was flattered that Diane was going to such lengths to share my story with the world, but I would have really appreciated ten minutes of advanced notice.

The next morning, I was on the front page of the local newspaper. I joked that Diane should become my personal promoter. She asked me how much I was paying and whether I could offer her benefits.

The article in Diane's local newspaper

That day we left her house for the Appalachian Trail Kickoff (ATKO), an annual event held at Amicalola Falls State Park. The Appalachian Trail Conservancy, hiking clubs, authors, vendors, AT experts, and newbie and veteran hikers alike congregate at the park to meet and greet other people in the hiking community and to hear AT-related news. I would have been excited to attend the event even if I hadn't been preparing to set off on the trail.

Amicalola Falls Lodge

Diane still had a good relationship with her ex-husband, and he paid for Diane and me to stay at the Amicalola Falls Lodge for one night. We checked in, then we drove to Amicalola Falls so I could register for the hike. On our way back to the lodge, we picked up a hitchhiker. A big grin spread across his face when I introduced myself to him.

"You're the hiker with one leg! I read about you online," he said.

It was flattering to be recognized. "That's me."

"I'm doing a documentary about AT thru-hikers. Do you mind if I interview you?" he asked.

I shrugged. "Why not?" I hadn't even started my thru-hike, but here I was giving my first interview.

Diane and I ate a huge breakfast the next morning before we attended the presentations of thru-hikers who'd walked the entire trail at some point in their lives. One of the presenters was Gene Epsy, a guy who had thru-hiked the AT back in 1951, well before most of the people in the room were even born. Gene was the second thru-hiker to complete the entire 2,200-mile hike. It only took him 123 days, and that was with no flashlight! He shared some fascinating tales of his months on the trail, and I felt so inspired when he handed the microphone to the next speaker. I wondered if I'd be able to finish the trail. Did I still have what it took to thru-hike the AT?

"Every accomplishment starts with the decision to try."
~ Gail Devers

Gene Epsy, one of the first AT thru-hikers

I said goodbye to Diane later that afternoon. She had to drive three hours to get back home. Right after she left, I met a woman named Joan, who recognized me from Facebook. She struck up a conversation about my strategy for the AT, my experiences on the PCT, and my backpack. She was curious to know how much my pack weighed. I didn't have an answer for her, so I found a scale and plopped my pack on it. The thing weighed twenty-four pounds with food but without water. Joan nodded her head approvingly, then she asked me if I had a trail name. When I said that I didn't, she told me that she thought I should be called Bionic Woman. I laughed and told her that another guy I'd met on Facebook had said the same thing. She said I should stick with it because it was unlikely that I'd ever find a more fitting name.

I thought I was going to have to pitch my tent that night, but Joan invited me to crash on her extra bed in her room at the lodge. "Trail magic" is a term that long-distance hikers use to describe a random act of kindness from total strangers on the trail. This was definitely trail magic, even if I wasn't officially on the trail yet.

Joan's kindness reminded me of another time that I benefitted from some trail magic. Back in 2002, I visited North America for the first time, landing in Vancouver, Canada. I didn't want to pay more than necessary to ship my gear, so before boarding the plane in Germany, I'd taken my bicycle apart to make sure my checked-in luggage didn't measure more than fifty-four linear inches (that's the sum of the length, width, and height of the bag). I collected my bag from baggage claim and found an empty corner. Then I took my gear out, so I could put my bicycle together. I spread everything in my bag all over the ground. It was almost dark, and I didn't want to leave the airport until my transportation was in one piece. I was trying to hurry so as not to draw any unwanted attention, but before I could finish putting the bicycle together, an airport security guard approached me. I probably would have gotten in trouble if I'd made such a mess in a German airport, and I expected him to yell at me.

Instead, the security guard said, "You look like you could use some help. Is there anything I can do for you?"

I was surprised by how friendly he was. "This is my first time in Vancouver," I said in my German-accented English. "Is there a campsite close? Maybe a youth hostel? Something cheap."

"Hold on a second," he said, and he walked away. Standing ten or fifteen feet from my sprawling mess, he made a call on his cell phone. A few minutes later, he walked over and handed his phone to me.

"Welcome to Vancouver," said the man's wife on the cell. "I hear you need a place to stay. We'd love to have you for the night. If you're interested."

I was stunned by the kindness of this man and his wife. I gratefully accepted, then handed the phone back to the security guard. He told me that he'd give me a ride to his house as soon as he was done with his shift. So, I finished putting my bicycle together, then I waited in baggage claim until he returned for me. We put my gear and my bicycle into the back of his truck, and we were off.

In the Vancouver airport in 2002

When I asked him how far he lived from the airport, he said, "Not far, eh."

Forty-five minutes later, we still hadn't arrived at his house, and I was getting nervous. I wondered if I'd mistaken homicidal scheming for kindness. I asked him how much farther we had to drive.

"Not far, eh" he said again in his Canadian accent.

"I think we have different meanings for 'not far,'" I said. "If you want to drive twenty miles in Germany, it's a big deal. And you must plan it in advance for at least several centuries."

He laughed and said, "About thirty more minutes. We're close, eh."

We eventually arrived safely at his house. His wife had prepared a lovely meal for the three of us, and she made up a bed for me in their spare room. They were awesome people, even if they didn't quite understand what "not far" means.

We had a nice breakfast the next morning, then the guy drove me to a port where I could catch a ferry to Vancouver Island. After I disembarked from the ferry, I rode my bicycle to Port Hardy, and I caught another ferry to Prince Rupert, close to the Inside Passage to Alaska. From there, I cycled to Alberta and then back to Vancouver. On my way back to Vancouver, I bought a huge coffee cup with the words "THANK YOU" printed on it. I took the cup and some pecan bird feeders I'd found in the middle of nowhere back to the couple's house to thank them for their generosity.

Taking a ride to Ferry Port with the Canadian couple and their dog

That's one of my all-time favorite trail magic stories. I tell it whenever I get the chance, especially when I happen across someone who has had a bad experience while traveling or hiking. Trail magic is out there, waiting for you. Just give it time, and eventually it will track you down.

8

A JOURNEY OF 2,200 MILES BEGINS WITH A SINGLE STEP

Thanks to the speakers who presented at the lodge, I got a late start on March 9, the day I set out on the trail. Not the Appalachian Trail, but the Appalachian Approach Trail, which departs from the summit of Amicalola Falls. It winds its way through a gorgeous forest sprinkled with rhododendron and filled with a variety of mossy trees. It's an incredibly scenic place to start such a long journey, and it stands in stark contrast to the barren desert that marks the beginning of the PCT on the California/Mexican border. At the start of the PCT, I wanted to hurry to lusher stretches of the trail, but I wanted to take my time through the Appalachian Approach Trail, to enjoy the splendor before my body started to ache and chafe. But I was also excited to get on the trail, officially.

It took me two days to reach the actual southern starting point of the AT on the Springer Mountain summit, about 8.5 miles from Amicalola Falls. Two plaques mark the southernmost blaze of the trail, and there is a trail register in a metal box full of names and messages from hikers who started their trek at Springer Mountain. I turned on my GoPro before putting my name on the list. It was a proud moment for me, one that seemed unimaginable fourteen months earlier.

I hiked fewer than three miles before I came to the first lean-to, a simple structure with a sloped roof, three walls, and wooden floors.

It was sunny that first day, but I'd have many rainy days on the AT, and those shelters would be lifesavers. Not only could I escape the cold rain for a while, but I could also remove my prosthetic leg and let my stump breathe. The skin and the scar tissue at the base of the limb were incredibly sensitive, especially in those early days on the trail, and I had to take frequent breaks like this one, so I could take care of my stump.

Those lean-tos were also a good place to meet other hikers. For those who don't know, there are three types of hikers on the AT. Day hikers are the most common. Then there are the section hikers, who only walk certain specific stretches of the AT. The least common type are people like me, the thru-hikers, who were doing—or at least trying to do—the whole kit and caboodle.

I spent my first night on the trail in one of those shelters. It's typical for section and thru-hikers to pile into the lean-tos at night, especially during the weekends, when there are more hikers on the trail. The structures vary in size, so they can hold different numbers of hikers, but even the smallest lean-to can usually accommodate six or more people. If there are more hikers in the area than can fit comfortably in the shelters, there are usually tent sites nearby. There would be many nights in the coming months when I'd have to pitch my tent next to one of those shelters, but there was room for me inside that night, so I staked a claim to an empty spot, rolled out my sleeping bag, and arranged my gear. I figured I could save time if I didn't have to set up and take down my tent. There was also a platform inside that I could sit on while I examined my stump to see how the scar tissue was holding up after a day of hiking.

There were some extra spaces in the lean-to that night, but one of the thru-hikers still set up his tent outside instead. As he was building a campfire, I asked him if I could join him. He waved me over and introduced himself. His trail name was Midnight. We struck up quite the conversation. He was an interesting guy, and it turned out that we had a lot in common. We were both thru-hikers, and we'd also both suffered traumatic injuries. He was a veteran of the War in Afghanistan, and he lost all his toes when an improvised explosive device (IED) detonated near him. Like me, his doctors had pumped him full of morphine and oxycodone to blunt the pain, and he also had a prescription to help him deal with his PTSD. At one point, he was taking more than ten pills a day, and like most people taking so many medications, he eventually became addicted. He said that his brain was usually so fogged up that he often didn't know what day of the week it was.

Showing off my prosthetic leg in a lean-to on the AT

Midnight's daughter eventually intervened. With tears in his eyes, he said that he'd be dead if she hadn't helped wean him off the medications. She slowly reduced the number of pills he was taking every day until, three months later, he was completely drug free. His story was both heartbreaking and heartwarming. And it also hit close to home. His tale of addiction easily could have been mine. While I was recovering from my fall, my doctor constantly asked me if I needed refills on my prescriptions. In fact, he often asked me if I needed a refill at the beginning of my visits, before he even asked me how I was doing. My previous experiences with pain medications back when I was a teenager recovering from that bicycle crash in Germany made me hypervigilant about opioids, and I stopped using my meds as soon as I possibly could, otherwise I might have been the one sitting by the fire talking about an addiction that nearly cost me my life.

Midnight's story reminded me of another one that I'd heard from a friend who'd once landed in jail for ten days for driving while intoxicated. While in jail, my friend learned about the death of another inmate in the same jailhouse. As I heard it told, the guy who died was in his twenties, and he had a wife, a child, and a good job. He was a very happy man until he was involved in a serious car accident that landed him in the hospital for several months. Like Midnight and me, he was given morphine in the hospital to help him deal with his physical pain. After he left, he was prescribed oxycodone, and soon enough he was hooked on opioids. When he finally ran out of refills, he turned to heroin. He was a full-blown heroin addict when he was arrested for possession of a Schedule 1 drug.

He went into withdrawal after his arrest. His condition became so bad that his body couldn't hold fluids. He was said to have pushed the emergency call button in his cell countless times. He pleaded for intravenous fluids, but the nurses who were supposed to be taking care of him told him that he would only receive an IV if it was absolutely necessary. Sadly, he died of dehydration, and all because the jail administration refused to shell out $20 for an IV bag that could have replenished his fluids. The jail was run by a for-profit corporation, and my friend believed that the staff were trying to cut costs to maximize profits.

After bonding over our stories of struggle, Midnight and I decided to hike together for a while, starting the next morning. Or maybe I should say that we decided to limp together because we were both in pain after that first day on the trail. This slow pace was difficult for me to swallow. Back when I hiked the PCT, no one ever passed me. My nickname on that trail had been Lean Mean Hiking Machine, and there were a couple times when I hiked more than forty miles in a single day. But now I was being passed by overweight people. The competitive athlete in me hated that I couldn't keep up with other thru-hikers, and I voiced my frustration to Midnight. He tried cheering me up, assuring me that I'd once again be a lean mean hiking machine by the time I reached Maine.

"NO PAIN, NO GAIN, NO RAIN NO MAINE!"

I joked. He liked that little rhyme, and it became our mantra while we hobbled along the trail that day.

I hiked with Midnight for the next couple days. We stuck together until we reached Neels Gap, a divide on the Blue Ridge Mountains. We stayed there overnight, and the next morning I was on my own again. I've always enjoyed the peace of solitary hiking, but I also missed Midnight after we parted. It's amazing how close you can feel to a person after hiking together for just a few days. Shared experiences, especially challenging ones, are like glue for kindred spirits.

Relaxing at the Low Gap Shelter after an eleven-mile day

Later that morning, I came to a trailhead. I noticed a straw hat blowing along the ground of the parking lot. I walked over and picked it up. It was identical to the one I'd worn on the PCT (I think it came from REI), and it was a small/medium, a perfect fit. I decided that the hat was a lucky talisman, and I pushed myself hard that day. I hiked eleven miles before I made camp that evening. That was my best day yet, and I was encouraged by the progress I was making.

The next day, I met a wonderful family of hikers who heaped praise on me for taking on the AT on a prosthetic leg. You're an inspiration because you live in the moment, they told me. You give new meaning to that old where-there's-a-will-there's-a-way adage, they said. Please keep us posted on Facebook, and let us know if there's anything you need, they insisted. This was becoming a recurring theme in my encounters with other hikers. When I told them, I was trying to hike all the way to Maine, they gushed with encouragement. While it was always nice to hear such kind words, it was also a little embarrassing when total strangers lavished me with compliments. But then those encouraging words also helped sustain me on difficult days.

The family that gave me a ride into town for my next resupply stop

I'd been on the trail for ten days before my stump really started to bother me. After limping along for much of the morning, I stopped to rest. I found a couple boulders covered with moist moss. After I sat down, I pressed the button to release the pin lock system on my prosthetic leg and breathed a sigh of relief as I pulled my limb from the socket. When I rolled down the liner that wrapped around my stump, I discovered a huge blood blister on the inside of what remained of my calf. Yikes! It was an ugly monster of a blister, and I knew I had to rupture it. The thing was going to pop any minute if I kept walking on it, and I didn't want that blood all over the liner inside the socket. So, I gritted my teeth and poked it with my fingernails. It burst like a water balloon, blood exploding everywhere. I pulled out my first aid kit, found some antibacterial alcohol to disinfect the wound and a bandage, and wrapped the bandage around my leg.

I needed to get off the trail for a couple days to let the wound heal, but I was four or five miles from a trailhead where I could hitchhike to a hostel. I slid my stump back into the socket and started down the trail. Every step was agony. I felt like I was walking on a spike each time I put weight on the bandaged leg. Eventually I made it to the trailhead. I sat on a guardrail on the side of the road, grabbed a bottle of water, and settled in for a long wait for a ride. But a van pulled up minutes later. On the side was a large decal that read "Hostel and Hiking Center." What luck! That was exactly where I intended to hitchhike.

When I arrived at the hostel, which was in Hiawassee, Georgia, I saw Midnight again. We hugged, then he gave me a frosty IPA, my favorite beer. I started to introduce myself to the other hikers, but I discovered that they all already knew who I was. Midnight had been at the hostel for the last two days, and he'd told them everything he knew about me. He said that he'd left the trail for the same reason I had: severe pain. The two days of rest had served his body well, and he was planning on hitchhiking back to the trailhead the next day. I told him that I'd met a couple who'd been waiting for a ride at the trailhead for well over an hour (they skipped the van ride to the hostel because they thought the owner was asking too much money for a forty-minute round-trip ride), so he should expect a long wait. But Midnight was a patient man, and he said that he didn't mind. After all, it wasn't like the AT was going anywhere, and he wasn't in a hurry to finish.

"You have to hike your own hike," he said. "It's all about the journey and not the destination, right? If I have to wait a little bit, that'll just give me more time to smell the roses."

I loved his optimism, and I was glad I'd bumped into him again, so we could spend some more time together.

I woke up early the next morning because my bunk bed was next to the kitchen, and I heard dishes clinking, the drip of fresh-brewed coffee, and the laughter of other hikers. I would like to have had a few more minutes of sleep, but then I also liked the idea of sitting around drinking coffee with a group of like-minded—and freshly showered—people. So, I got up to search for my liner to put on my stump. When I looked down at my leg, I saw that it had swollen to several times its normal size, and it had turned all kinds of angry colors. Red, yellow, purple—it was an irate rainbow. My limb clearly hated me. There was no way I was going to be able to squeeze it back into the socket, so I hopped to the kitchen on one leg to get a cup of coffee and to say hi to everyone.

When the other hikers spotted my inflamed limb, their faces turned serious. One guy, whose trail name was Yogi Bear, thought I should see a doctor. I hated to admit it, especially since I still had such a long way to get to Maine, but I knew he was right. There was no way I could continue until I saw a medical professional.

I finished my coffee and hopped back into my room to find my hiking poles. I used them to limp my way to the hostel's office, where I found the owner. I asked him if I could get a ride to a clinic to see a doctor. He said he'd be happy to take me. When I went back to my room to look for my wallet, I couldn't find it. I emptied my pack, checked in the bed, searched the floor, but it was nowhere to be found. My ID, my driver's license, my bank cards, my cash—everything was gone. When it rains, it pours.

---

*"Be thankful for each new challenge,
because it will build your strength and character."*
~ Unknown

Midnight came to my door to tell me that the owner was ready to take me into town. When I said I couldn't find my wallet, he told me that he would be happy to give me some money. He reached into his wallet and pulled out $100. I told him that he was being too generous, that I couldn't possibly accept so much money, but he insisted.

"The trail provides," he said. "Just pay it forward someday." I was touched, and I turned away to hide the tears in my eyes In town, I saw a doctor who prescribed antibiotics and crutches. The owner of the hostel then drove me to the pharmacy. I handed him the $100 bill at the drive through. When the pharmacist gave him the change, he put it into his pocket and told me that he was keeping the money to cover the cost of my hostel stay. I was mad as a wildcat. I told him that I needed that cash to buy crutches and food. I had money in the bank, I argued, and as soon as I got replacement cards, I'd pay him what I owed. Eventually he agreed to give me the change, minus $20 for my first night. I couldn't believe this guy. It felt like he was kicking me while I was down, and I wanted to get out of his car as soon as possible.

At a store that sold medical supplies, I discovered that I didn't have enough money for regular-sized crutches—thanks to the owner of the hostel—so I had to buy a pair meant for children. They were way too short, but at least they were better than my hiking poles, which didn't make hopping around on one leg easy.

When I got back to the hostel, Yogi Bear, the other thru-hiker, felt bad for me for having to use such undersized crutches, so he found a beat-up old broom and broke it into pieces to make the crutches more height appropriate for me. The owner found out that we'd destroyed the broom later that day, and true to form, he yelled at us. That cheapskate was the reason I had to buy those kid-sized crutches, so I didn't feel bad about destroying a ratty old broom, but Yogi Bear bought a new one the next day. I think he probably did it for me, so the owner of the hostel wouldn't throw me out over a $10 broom. I'd met so many great people on the trail to that point, but this guy reminded me that not everyone was in my corner, not everyone was as selfless as Midnight and Yogi Bear.

I called Diane later that day. I'd left a spare bank card and my German driver's license at her house in Georgia, and I asked her to overnight them to me at the hostel. Besides mailing my cards to me, she also sent some extra cash. She's such a sweetheart, and her kindness more than made up for the hostel owner's meanness.

Later, I called my prosthetist in Denver to tell him that the pin-lock system was definitely not working out for me. He said that he thought an air-suction system might be a better option, which was exactly what an adaptive snowboarder had told me while I was skiing in Colorado during my visit to my prosthetist to get a leg for the AT. He told me that he'd contact a prosthetist in Columbia, South Carolina.

That was a good solution since Columbia was only a few hours away by car.

I had to wait until the swelling decreased, so I decided to get a ride into a town called Gainesville, and from there I could catch a Greyhound bus to Columbia. I stayed in a motel that night. It was significantly more expensive than the hostel I'd just left, but at least I didn't have to deal with that scrooge any more. And it was nice knowing that I wouldn't be awoken at dawn by early-bird hikers.

But as I lay in bed that night, the pain in my swollen leg became unbearable. I tossed and turned for a while, hoping that I'd eventually fall asleep, but my leg wouldn't stop throbbing long enough to allow my brain to shut down for the night. I gave up after lying there for a couple hours and decided to kill some time by posting pictures and a couple paragraphs on Facebook via my cell phone. Just minutes after I posted the update, a woman named Brooke, who'd given me a ride just days before, sent me a message, telling me that I was in her hometown and that she was concerned about my leg. It turned out that she was a certified nurse practitioner, and she wasn't working the next day. She asked me if she could pick me up and take me to her clinic. Talk about trail magic!

When she examined my leg the following morning, she said that she was pleasantly surprised. The photos I'd posted the night before were just three days old, but my leg had already healed significantly. She said that it looked much better than she had anticipated, which was a relief to her because she thought she was going to have to recommend that I quit my hike or risk having my limb amputated above the knee. She also said that my rapid healing was proof that I had an excellent immune system, which was proof that I had a healthy, balanced diet. Most of her patients ate crap like processed food with lots of sugar and salt.

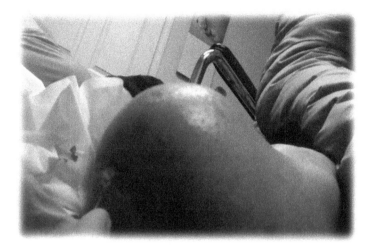

The certified nurse practitioner inspecting my limb

She was right about most people, but I wasn't most people. I'd been trained as a chef, and I'd been an athlete almost my whole life. I was well versed in the importance of a good diet. When I resupplied my food stock in town, I picked up avocados and other fruits, and I bought canned sardines, scallops, ginger, trail mix, and garlic. I also liked to shop in the Asian section, so I could get wasabi, miso-soup, whole wheat noodles, seaweed, and whatever else I could find. Grocery bills are a little higher when you buy healthy food, but it's less expensive in the long run because you don't have to see a doctor as often. She said that she wished that her patients who suffered from obesity and type 2 diabetes shared my philosophy about food.

Before we left the clinic, Brooke invited me to stay with her family for a couple days until the swelling subsided.

That invitation also included a one-day visit to Atlanta, where she was running a marathon the following day. I enjoyed cheering her on, almost as much as I enjoyed the fried green tomatoes that we ate at her favorite Italian restaurant after the marathon. I'd heard about that Southern delicacy for years, but this was the first time I had an opportunity to try it. It definitely lived up to its reputation.

Recovering with Brooke's family in their home

A traditional Southern meal after Brooke's marathon

After a couple more days, the swelling in my stump decreased enough for me to squeeze it into the socket, which allowed me to toss out the crutches and walk on my prosthetic again. Before leaving Gainesville, I found a Couchsurfing host who was willing to put me up for a few nights in Columbia. Then I bought a ticket on a Greyhound bus, and I was off to South Carolina. I hadn't envisioned doing so much traveling by bus or car while hiking the AT but based on the recommendation I received from my prosthetist in Denver, I was confident that the prosthetist I was scheduled to meet in Columbia would help get me back on the trail as quickly as possible.

The next morning, I met the prosthetist, a guy named Bobby Latham. He picked me up and took me to his clinic, Bulow Ortho-pedics. I hadn't budgeted for a trip to a prosthetist while on the AT, and I would have had a hard time coming up with the money for a new socket if I hadn't found a sponsor in Boa and Click Medical, a company that makes the Boa System, a really cool way to tighten shoes without shoelaces. They offered to pay for the socket and for the prosthetist's labor. More trail magic!

Bobby made a cast of my leg. When it dried, he sent it to the company that created the socket. He told me I'd have to wait about a week to receive it. I understand that these things don't get made overnight, but I was itching to get back on the trail. I couldn't imagine sitting around doing nothing for another week, so I decided that I was going to jump back on the AT with a temporary test socket. It wasn't made from carbon fiber, but it was wrapped with sturdy tape, and it only needed to last me a week, until Bobby mailed the new socket to me somewhere on the trail.

Before leaving Columbia, I stayed one more night with my Couch-surfing host. To show my appreciation, I cooked my host a German dish called Spätzle, which is an egg-noodle pasta popular in Southern Germany. I made it from scratch, and I topped it off with fried onions, bacon, and cheese. The dish has about 10,000 calories in it, which is perfect for thru-hikers who burn at least that many calories every day on the trail, but it's probably a bit much for everyone else.

Rather than sitting on another Greyhound bus for twelve hours the next day, I got smart and called Dorothy from Adidas. I told her about my predicament and asked her if it would be possible for Adidas to sponsor me for the cost of a rental car, so I could get back on the trail. She told me that they'd absolutely take care of the rental car for me, and she insisted that I call her again if I needed anything else on the trail.

I picked up the car a couple hours later, and I headed back to Georgia. I intended to return to the trail at the exact same spot I'd left it, near Hiawassee. Although I didn't like the idea of giving that tightwad at the hostel any more of my money, I decided to stay there that night. Oh well. One more night wasn't going to kill me.

About halfway to Georgia, I received a phone call from an online radio personality who wanted to interview me. It was pouring rain, so I pulled over. Sitting on the shoulder of the road in the rental car, I gave my first formal interview. I was a bit nervous, but it was also an adrenaline rush. I wasn't walking the AT for the attention, but I have to admit that the attention was really flattering.

After I hung up, it occurred to me that I didn't have to stay at the same hostel, I had options. If Adidas was willing to sponsor me for the rental car, then maybe they'd be willing to pay for a night in a hotel. So, I called Dorothy again at the Adidas offices in LA and asked her if Adidas could help me. Once again, she came through for me. Rather than staying in a hostel owned by a jerk, I crashed in a hotel. Thank you, Dorothy and Adidas.

9

ON THE TRAIL AGAIN

I had a run of good luck for about forty trail miles, until I reached Franklin, North Carolina. One of the screws on the bottom of my socket wiggled loose, which made walking difficult. My prosthetic was built with metric screws, and of course I could only find standard screws in the hardware store I visited. It's frustrating that the US refuses to use the metric system.

"But where there is a will, there is a way."

I went to an auto repair shop in the hope that they might have what I was looking for. Unfortunately, they didn't, but the owner of the shop offered to make a new thread for me that would take standard screws. He worked on my prosthetic for about two hours. He did a marvelous job, and he didn't ask me to pay a single cent. What a great guy!

The auto mechanic who fixed my prosthetic leg

Not long after I left the auto shop, I contacted Dorothy from Adidas and asked her to send the owner of the auto shop a thank you gift for helping me. I also asked her if she could send something to Diane, my friend who was acting as my supply person, and to a guy at Neels Gap who'd helped me mount my GoPro camera on my backpack. Dorothy sent everything I requested, and I sent her several memory cards full of film footage for their documentary.

I left Franklin and pushed on. The air-suction socket of the temporary prosthetic was working fine now, and my stump no longer caused me as much pain. I hiked a fairly uneventful hundred miles before deciding to take a little detour to a town in Tennessee called Gatlinburg. Other hikers I'd met along the way told me that I should avoid Gatlinburg because it was nothing but a tourist trap ("If you like Disneyland, then you'll like Gatlinburg," one hiker had told me), but I was craving a little distraction at that point. So, I got a ride from the trailhead in the back of a pickup truck. The cool breeze blowing through my hair felt refreshing after slogging away on the trail that day.

At a hotel in Gatlinburg, I met another thru-hiker, a woman who was traveling with a service dog. Her trail name was Almost Triple Crowner because she'd finished two of the three major American hikes. In the hiking world, the Triple Crown refers to the Pacific Crest Trail, the Continental Divide Trail, and the Appalachian Trail. The total mileage for all three trails is more than 7,900 miles, which is almost 42,000,000 feet! Completing the Triple Crown is a big deal to hikers, and not many people accomplish the feat in a lifetime.

That night I shared a room with Almost Triple Crowner. At some point before we turned in for the night, I asked why she had a service dog. She offered a long, meandering explanation that I couldn't follow. I'd heard that some people fake medical conditions, so they can get a service dog, and I wondered if she might be one of them. I immediately scolded myself for harboring such a nasty thought, but later I learned from other hikers that she was known to be a sketchy person. Some hikers who'd been on the PCT with her told me that she was a "yellow trailblazer," meaning that she'd hitched rides and skipped big sections of the trail, which is a no-no for hikers claiming to have completed the entire trail. I wasn't going to condemn her based on rumors, but I will say that I wasn't shocked to hear that people were calling her a cheater behind her back.

The next day, Almost Triple Crowner asked me about aqua blazing from Virginia to West Virginia along the Shenandoah River. Aqua blazing is a form of "hiking" that involves traveling by a waterway that runs near the trail (for those who don't know, true thru-hikers usually backtrack after finishing an aqua blaze and get back on the trail where they left it). She told me she'd found a packable rubber boat that could be shipped to her on the trail. I told her I was thinking about doing it myself, but I'd definitely do it in a kayak. I tried to tell her that a rubber boat wouldn't last long on the rocky-bottomed river, but she was determined that it would work.

That same day, I met another thru-hiker named Square Bag, a guy who was working on his second attempt to hike the AT. He'd picked up his name from the square bag he wore around his hips. We hit it off instantly, and together we went down to the strip in Gatlinburg and took advantage of the free moonshine tasting in one of the shops, where he convinced the owner to "sponsor" me with a bottle of moonshine.

"The Bionic Woman is famous!" he exclaimed. "She can advertise it on the trail to other hikers."

And that was exactly what I did when I got back on the trail. After a long day that included lots of stops to put ointment on my stump to prevent skin irritation, I met a guy named Scotch in a lean-to shelter. While we were eating dinner that night, we sat around sharing shots of moonshine and scotch with other hikers, and I was happy for that unique form of sponsorship.

Moonshine tasting in Gatlinburg, Tennessee

Drinking moonshine with Scotch

I made decent time in the days that followed, and before I knew it, I'd arrived in a town called Hot Springs, roughly 270 miles from the starting point in Amicalola Falls. I'd hiked about an eighth of the AT. I was definitely making progress, even if I wasn't traveling nearly as quickly as I'd traveled on the PCT. But then I really shouldn't have been comparing my AT hike to my PCT hike. Besides my stump slowing me down, the trails were also very different. There are lots of switchbacks on the PCT, but hikers call the AT a rollercoaster because it goes up and down, and it's much more physically taxing, especially with all the rocks and boulders you have to hike over and around. On the other hand, the AT is far less remote than the PCT, so you don't have to carry as much food. And I knew that if my prosthetic gave me any trouble on the AT, help at a trailhead wasn't far off.

I picked up my new socket from a post office in Hot Springs. Using the tools included in the package, I mounted my Grateful Dead socket on my prosthetic foot. The new socket was an air-suction system, and it was much better than the old pin-lock system because it prevented rubbing on my scar tissue. I was very pleased that I'd taken time off to meet with Bobby in Columbia.

I was no longer shy about calling Dorothy to inquire about sponsorship, so while I was in Hot Springs, I decided to ask her if Adidas would pay for a massage and a soak in the springs. When she said that they were, once again, happy to help, I practically ran to the massage center. My therapist was a guy about my age, and he was in excellent condition. I'd gained a lot of muscle strength since starting on the trail, but those muscles were tight and knotted now. He loosened them up, then I took a long soak in the hot springs. I was in hiker's heaven that day.

I settled into a nice routine over the next hundred miles. I hiked between nine and twelve miles, depending on the trail conditions. Although I loved my new socket, my stump was still swollen at the end of every day, but the Boa Dial System allowed me to release some of the pressure.

Still, there were days when I was in considerable pain by late morning, and I often hiked the last two-thirds of the day with tears in my eyes. I credit my ability to move past the pain to all the years I devoted to athletics. I'd learned a long time ago that the only way to become a better athlete is to push beyond your comfort zone by accepting and living with the pain, knowing that the pain will eventually go away. My weeks on the AT had made my body stronger. I stopped taking pain medication every day, and I felt like I was becoming my old self again, the person I'd been before I nearly died in Utah. As an athlete, I knew that once you've developed muscle strength, it's much easier to regain that strength after you've lost it. All the years of hard workouts had paid off.

Midnight, the hiker I'd traveled with in Georgia, was right: when I reached my final destination, I would feel the way I did before my accident.

With that positive thought in mind, I pushed on. I pushed past the pain, past the goddamn rocks, the boulders, and the rollercoaster, the constant ups and downs.

Vista in Virginia

In Virginia, about 380 miles into my hike, I ran into Yogi Bear again, the guy who'd destroyed that broom to fix my crutches back in Hiawassee, Georgia. I met him at Lake Watauga, where a group of hikers were swimming and barbecuing. They invited me to join them, and I gladly jumped in. As always, my body—especially my stump—was aching, and the thought soaking for several hours made be deliriously happy. Later in the day, after we had our fill of barbecue and swimming, we all inflated our Therm-a-Rest sleeping pads and took them into the lake for some serious relaxing. "Therm-a-Rest blazing" was what one of the hikers called it.

"Therm-a Rest blazing" with Yogi Bear, Me and two other thru-hikers at Lake Watauga, Virginia

I didn't do much hiking for the rest of that day. After spending so much time pampering my muscles, I just couldn't motivate myself to get back on the trail so soon. I decided to get a good night's rest, so I could jump back on the trail first thing in the morning. But that plan didn't exactly pan out for me. Pain in my leg awoke me up all night, every hour or so. I woke up in misery three or four times before I packed up my gear, put on my prosthetic, and my trail runners, and turned on my headlamp. I'd done many night hikes on the PCT, but this was my first one on the AT. Being on the trail at night was amazing. The scenery was completely transformed. I was in the so-called green tunnel, which is what hikers call the portion of the AT that cuts through the woods. It was exciting to see the glowing eyes of the animals on and around the trail. The experience was so serene, so calming. I love running into other hikers, especially those who are full of positive energy, but there was something special about knowing that it was just the wildlife and me out there.

Those glowing eyes reflecting light from my headlamp reminded me of an experience I had in West Virginia back in 2003, when I was cycling across the US. I pitched my tent near a lake and ate dinner, then I sat down to smoke a bowl of herb. The feel of the herb in my blood, the sound of the wind blowing through the pine needles, the smell of the breeze blowing over the lake—they were so relaxing. After I finished smoking my bowl, I was too tired to get up and do the dishes. I just crawled into my tent and went to sleep.

Sometime in the middle of the night, I woke up because I sensed someone standing next to me. I could feel body heat through the tent wall. I was convinced that someone was trying to steal my gear. As I searched for my headlamp, I yelled at the intruder.

"Get the hell out of here! I don't have anything worth stealing!"

I finally found my headlamp under my Therm-a-Rest, and I put it on my head, my hands shaking. I turned it on, unzipped my tent, and then screamed myself hoarse. A black bear stood inches away, breathing its animal stink into my face. The only time I've ever screamed louder was when I was falling from that cliff in Utah.

I was staring right into the black bear's face. I was terrified, and I was certain that the beast was going to kill me. But my earsplitting scream must have frightened the animal because it ran off into the forest. I watched it go, trying to decide which way I should run. The bear was some distance from my camp when it turned around and stared back at me, its eyes glowing with reflected light. The shimmering orbs hovered there for an instant, then disappeared into the night.

I grabbed my tent as fast as possible and hurried to the park's official campsite, where I felt safer. I set up my tent and tried to settle my nerves. I wondered what had drawn the animal to my campsite. I was running through a list of possible reasons when I remembered my beef stew in my cooking pot. I'd been lazy about cleaning up after myself that night, and the smell of my dinner was practically a written invitation to the bear. I knew better than to leave food lying around in bear country. I'd let my guard down in a peaceful moment, and it nearly got me killed. That was definitely another one of my nine lives gone.

Back on the AT, I continued my night hike until about 4 a.m., when I decided to stop and make camp. I pitched my tent and fell asleep immediately. My late-night hike did the trick because I slept like a log, and I didn't wake up once with pain in my leg.

The sound of other hikers awoke me the next morning. Before putting the liner back onto my stump, I slathered the limb with ointment meant to protect my sensitive skin, especially the scar tissue on the bottom of the stump, which wasn't completely healed yet from the wound caused by my old pin-lock system. When I popped open that blood blister in Georgia, bacteria seeped into my open scar tissue and created the infection that caused my leg to swell to four times its normal size. I was doing everything I could to prevent another bump in the road like the one that had taken me off the trail for twelve days.

When I stepped out of my tent, I found that I was surrounded by seven women hikers. Including me, there were eight women in camp and only one man. I'm not sure if this abundance of women on the AT was a sign that hiking was becoming less of a male-dominated activity, or if the male-to-female ratio was just very different on the AT than on the PCT. Back in 2006 when I was hiking the PCT, the vast majority of the hikers I met were men. Occasionally I'd run into a couple, but only rarely did I cross paths with a woman on her own. Being surrounded by so many women was a nice change of pace.

As usual, I cooked my breakfast on my Pepsi-can stove. Besides drinking coffee to get me going, I ate whole grain oats with nuts, raisins, and powdered milk, and I added wheat grains and flax seeds for extra fiber. I was still on an opioid called tramadol to cope with my pain, and one of the side effects is constipation. Life on the trail is already difficult enough without blocked bowels, so I did what I could to stay regular. Maintaining a healthy diet while hiking long distances is difficult enough without a severe disability, but it's especially hard while managing pain with opioids.

"Your disability does not define you.
Your strength and courage does."
~ Unknown

Because I hiked so late into the night, I didn't step onto the trail until late morning. Not long after I started hiking, I met a couple whose collective trail name was Peanut Butter and Jelly. They were hiking with a puppy they'd rescued from a shelter. The woman, Jelly, tied the puppy's leash around her waist and let the ultra-hyper dog pull her along the trail. I thought it was a brilliant idea. I told her how impressed I was with her ingenuity, and she told me how impressed she was that I was hiking on a prosthetic leg. We hiked together for a bit, then she stopped me and tied the leash around my waist. The dog took off up a hill, pulling me along. It felt as if the puppy were relieving me of about a quarter of my body weight. That was the easiest hiking I'd ever done.

The three of us—four if you count the dog—traveled together that day until we came to the property of a guy who accommodates hikers in a spare hut next to his house. He had a sign on the trailhead that said that his lodgings were only for thru-hikers. Section hikers, day hikers, and yellow blazers were forbidden from staying there overnight.

Hiking with Peanut Butter and his dog

When we arrived, I saw Almost Triple Crowner talking to the owner of the property. The guy turned away from her and said in an animated voice, "The Bionic Woman! I read about you online!"

Almost Triple Crowner's face twisted into a scowl. "I guess the Bionic Woman's story is way more interesting than mine," she snapped. Then she stormed off with her service dog.

I was disappointed that Almost Triple Crowner was turning our hikes into a competition, especially after we'd shared a room. I wouldn't call her a friend, but we'd hung out a little. And the last time I'd seen her, she helped me get a refill on some pain medication. It irritated me that she seemed so upset to see me.

The owner of the property introduced himself, and we chatted for a bit. I asked him about crashing in his hut, and he told me that my stay was free. That saved me $20! I wouldn't exactly call myself a famous hiker, but it felt awesome to get some recognition for doing something out of the ordinary, something that the doctors and even some friends and family said was impossible.

In a hiker hut with Almost Triple Crowner, Peanut Butter, and Jelly

While I was eating breakfast the next morning, Peanut Butter and Jelly asked me if I'd like to hike with them that day. They'd arranged to stay overnight with a friend who lived near Damascus, Virginia, and they'd gotten permission from the guy to invite me to his house. I love meeting new people, and I thought it would be nice to take a shower and spend a night in a real bed, so I accepted their offer. We packed up our gear and headed out.

Their friend met us in trailhead parking lot. The guy was fifty-something and super friendly. He arrived with an icebox full of frosty microbrewery beer, and he didn't exactly have to twist my arm to take one. We had a little tailgate party in the back of his pickup truck. Afterwards, we drove to his house, took a very long hot shower, and went to dinner at his favorite Italian restaurant. That was an awesome night away from the trail.

The next couple days, I did some wandering off the trail to check out the wild ponies I found at a highlands ranch. They weren't timid at all. You could walk right up to them and show them a little love with a rub on the nose or a scratch on the ear. They seemed to like all people, but I suspect that hikers are probably their favorite type of human, especially thru-hikers. Most of us don't bathe every day, so we accumulate layers of sweat all over our bodies. We're essentially walking salt licks for the ponies. As soon I approached them, one of them licked my arm while another one licked my good leg. In most parts of the world, you'd have to pay good money for a tongue bath like that!

Ponies giving a tongue bath at a highlands ranch

Later that day, I ran into a guy who'd given me a ride a couple weeks earlier. He told me that he was looking for another thru-hiker to bring to Damascus for Trail Days, an annual three-day festival celebrating the AT and the people who love it. It sounded fun, and I liked the idea of hanging around Damascus for a few extra days.

Life often has a way of taking me in unexpected directions. Sometimes it takes me to places like Damascus, where I met incredible people and had unique experiences. Other times it puts me in much less desirable positions. Take my fall in Utah, for example. Before my accident, I'd been planning to join the Navy Reserve, but I needed to pass the Armed Services Vocational Aptitude Battery (ASVAB) test to enter into the services. The first time I took the test, I failed. It kicked my butt, plain and simple. But because I'm not the type to walk away from a challenge, I took a class at a local community college that was supposed to help me pass the test. I studied the stupid standard measurement system that only Americans use, and I memorized lots of really "useful" English vocabulary words like "ossify," "concupiscence," and "skullduggery." But even after weeks and weeks of studying, I failed that damn test again. I became so frustrated after getting my test results back the second time that I decided to take my friends up on their offer to accompany them on a canyoneering trek in Utah. I let life take me where it wanted me to go, and apparently it wanted me sprawled out on the rocky floor of a canyon and near death. I was doing everything I could do to become a Navy reservist, but I ended up as an amputee, even before I could join the military to get deployed to a war battlefield where I could lose a leg as well. I've learned that you can only plan so far. Much of what happens in life is completely out of your control. That was a hard lesson, to accept.

"Dont' be afraid to fail. Be afraid not to try."
~ Michael Jordan

For any AT hikers in the area during Trail Days, I highly recommend attending. If you're on the trail, there is no shortage of trail angels on the AT around Damascus during the festival (for those who don't know, trail angels are people who deliver heaping helpings of trail magic), so it's easy for hikers to get rides into town. Keep your eyes open for Miss Janet, the most famous of the trail angels. She always has a smile on her face, and she drives hikers in her van back and forth between the AT and Damascus. She also follows the "bubble" of hikers and helps whenever possible.

Hanging out with Miss Janet   Miss Janet's van

I checked into the Woodchuck Hostel, where I pitched my tent among many other tents. The owner of the Woodchuck had hiked the AT by himself several years earlier, so he understood the needs of hikers perfectly. I enjoyed my stay there.

That same day, I received a message from a friend I'd met a couple weeks earlier. He'd driven more than forty miles to the AT to resupply me with a new sleeping pad after something sharp popped mine. My battered body made sleep difficult enough even with the pad; I never would have fallen asleep without one. In Damascus, my friend arranged an interview for me with a local TV station called WCYB Channel 5. It was my second formal interview after the radio interview weeks earlier. I was excited, my first TV interview, it went very well, and it increased my profile on the AT.

Thanks to that interview, I received some sponsorships from a few of the many vendors at Trail Days. A company called Kelty gave me a free summer sleeping bag, and a German company called Deuter Sport supplied me with a free backpack. And Hennessy Hammock gave me an ultra-lightweight hammock to help me sleep at night. I went straight to the hostel and set it up at the shelter. I couldn't wait to test it out that night.

My first TV interview in Damascus during Trail Days

The next morning, I saw Mr. Hennessy, and I gave him a big hug. That night had been the first time on the trail that I hadn't woken up in pain. Sleeping in that hammock was infinitely better than sleeping on my Therm-a-Rest on the ground, and I decided that it was time to replace my tent with a Hennessey hammock.

I wasn't the only hiker at Trail Days who benefitted from the kindness of the people of Damascus. A local church made some significant contributions to the event, and hundreds of hikers received free meals. Volunteers gave complimentary foot massages to hikers, and there was even a place for hikers to get free haircuts. Damascus is a special town, and the people went way above and beyond the call of duty during Trail Days. Like I said before, I highly recommend the event to any hikers who are planning to be near Damascus in May.

A free foot massage in Damascus during Trail Days

On the final day of the festival, the town held a giant parade, and everyone present was invited to participate. Men dressed like women; women dressed like stuffed animals. Adults behaved like children. Everybody who was hiking the AT walked in groups like we were a graduating class. When the parade ended and the sun set, we had a giant campfire. Some danced around it like prehistoric fire worshippers. Others sat around drinking beer and telling stories. It was one of my favorite experiences on the trail.

Hanging out with some cross-dressing hikers at Trail Days in Damascus

I got back on the trail the next day, armed with all my new treasures from the vendors who had so generously sponsored me. Just minutes after I started hiking that morning, I came across a group of people, including a paramedic, bent over a hiker. The story I heard was that a woman had fallen on the trail and dislocated a disc in her back. Lucky for her, she was hiking with others, and one of her friends ran to the nearest lean-to shelter and found three more hikers. After returning to the spot of the accident, they used their hiking poles and sleeping bags to create a makeshift stretcher to carry the woman several miles to the nearest trailhead, where a paramedic started giving her first aid. Who knows what would have happened to that poor woman if her friends hadn't taken such good care of her until the paramedic arrived. I later heard through the hiker grapevine that her injury was so severe that she had to abandon her plans to thru-hike the AT. I really empathized with her.

Injured hiker on the trail

That evening, I came to a zip-line that crossed the river and landed on the private property of a trail angel who let hikers stay overnight in tents. It was dark when I arrived at the zip-line, and I didn't spend much time studying it or considering my trajectory. I jumped on with my backpack, and with a big push, I was zipping down the line. Toward the other side of the river, I landed in the water, and my prosthetic stuck to the zip-line. I'm lucky that the water wasn't very deep and that there wasn't a strong current, otherwise I might have drowned with my backpack tied around my body. Using all my core strength, I managed to pull myself up and to get my prosthetic untangled. I arrived at the trail angel's house soaking wet.

Zip-line across the river

Generally speaking, I'd give just about anything to have my leg back, but I have to admit that there are times when having a disability is an asset. When the guy whose property I'd just zipped onto saw me dripping and limping, he invited me to take a shower at his house. And after I cleaned up, he handed me a cold beer. A thru-hiker is grateful for every gift, but especially thankful when that gift is cold beer. It hit the spot after a long day of hiking.

Later that night, I thought a lot about my mishap on the zip-line. I was lucky that only my pride was hurt. Things definitely could have turned out differently. I like to think of myself as a careful person. When I go out adventuring with friends, I'm usually the one insisting that we double- and triple-check our gear, but on occasion I have momentary lapses in judgment, like on the zip-line that day. Or in that harness in Utah. Or on my bicycle when I was a teenager.

Then there was the time I tried to cross a river in the Sierra Nevada while I was hiking the PCT in 2006. There had been a record snowfall the previous winter, and there was a lot of runoff from snowmelt that spring. As a result, the rivers that are fed by the melting snow grew wider, deeper, and faster. When I came to a river up in Northern California, it wasn't very deep, but it looked like it was moving fairly quickly. To test how fast the current was moving, I stuck the tip of my hiking pole into the water. It nearly ripped the pole out of my hand. That water was moving at a good clip, but the river was shallow, so I decided to risk crossing on foot. I secured my hiking poles in my pack, then I stepped into the river. The water immediately swept me off my feet and ripped off one of my Keen hiking sandals. In any other river, my biggest concern would have been running into a boulder or being gashed by a root or something sharp below the waterline, but on this river the gravest threat—the threat that could have literally sent me to my grave—was the waterfall I was barreling toward.

I panicked and swam for the shore. I'm a former triathlete, and I consider myself a good swimmer, but I didn't make much progress because my backpack was strapped around my body and the current was strong. I rolled over onto my back, so I could see downstream. I noticed a tree branch sticking out over the water near shore. I paddled in that direction as the water pushed me downstream. When I was close to the branch, I reached out and grabbed it in a death grip with one hand, then I latched onto it with my other hand. For a moment,

I wondered if I had the strength to pull myself out of the water, but I sure as hell wasn't going over that waterfall without a fight. Teeth gritted, I pulled and clawed my way out of the water. It took all my upper body strength to escape the current, and when I was finally out, lying on my back on the river bank and trying to catch my breath, I thanked my lucky stars for the narrow escape. Then I scolded myself for being so careless. That was yet another of my nine lives gone.

Crossing a river on the PCT in 2006   Waterfall on a river on the PCT

As I lay in my sleeping bag that night on the AT, thinking back on my brushes with death, I realized that I needed to be more careful in the future. The problem is that when you live on the edge, when you jump out of airplanes and rappel down cliffs on a regular basis, you don't have much room for error, and a momentary lapse in judgment can quickly put an end to your days of adventuring. It's not enough to be vigilant 99% of the time. I needed to make sure I was seeing to my safety every time I was doing something risky.

10

AQUA BLAZING

I got back on the trail the next morning. There were several other hikers waiting to cross the river on the zip-line when I arrived, so I had a wait for my turn. When it came time for me to cross, I took care to get to the other shore safely. I made sure to avoid making the same dumb mistake a second time.

Later that day, I hiked up Catawba Mountain to McAfee Knob, a finger of mountain that juts out over the Catawba Valley 3,400 feet below. I could see hills and mountains and valleys for miles and miles. It's a gorgeous scenic point that makes you acutely aware of your smallness as an individual, of the tiny piece of space you occupy on this planet. It's both inspiring and intimidating. You feel important for having witnessed such grandeur, but also insignificant for the same reason. I visited the knob during the middle of the day, but I can imagine how much more impressive it would have been at night, with all those billions and billions of stars and galaxies to contemplate overhead. There's a reason that McAfee Knob is one of the most famous and most photographed spots on the AT.

After I descended Catawba Mountain and got back on the trail, I met a hiker called High Noon. He was walking with a sweet German Shepherd mix. We hiked together for a while before he invited me to take a "safety break" with him (in other words, to smoke a bowl with him). I happily joined him. It felt wonderful to distract my mind from the pain that plagued my body and to forget about how much farther I still had to hike that day before setting up camp. We smoked that bowl together, then he got back on the trail and hightailed it north. I lagged behind him, but I caught up with him again later that day because he'd stopped for another safety break. I smoked with him a second time, and we talked about aqua blazing on the South River, which wasn't far from his home in Virginia. That meant that we'd have access to a car to transport the kayaks to the river. Trail magic!

For much of the week before, I'd been trying to figure out a way to rent or buy a kayak in Waynesboro, Virginia, which is the entry point for the South River. I found a place that rented kayaks, but they'd only let you travel down a third of the river, and they were asking way more than I could afford on my budget. The last time I resupplied at a Walmart, I found $250 kayaks on the store floor. High Noon said that he was definitely interested in buying one and aqua blazing with me, but we still had about a hundred miles to hike before we arrived at Waynesboro. I knew there was no way I could keep up with him and his energetic dog, so we agreed to part ways and to keep in touch on Facebook and on our cell phones. He offered to pick me up whenever I gave the word.

The school house with snacks

High Noon and his dog

Before we went our separate ways, we emerged from the green tunnel and walked into a wide-open pasture. We decided to take a break—a break-break, not a safety break—near a school building that was probably a couple hundred years old. When we peeked inside through the glass-paneled front door, we saw a box with a sign on it that read, "Thru-hikers only." Our curiosity got the better of us, and we turned the knob on the door to see if it was locked. It wasn't; it swung right open. We called out a few times, and when no one answered, we walked over to the box. Inside we found sodas and candy bars and, to my surprise, real food like bananas and apples. Woohoo!

While we were eating our snacks, I pulled out my cell phone. I hadn't had internet access for days, and I was curious to see if we had reception. I saw that I had a couple bars, so I jumped onto my Facebook account. I discovered that another hiker had found my GoPro camera, which I'd lost in Damascus during Trail Days. A hiker named Ron had stumbled upon the camera and had purchased a power cord, so he could charge it to find out who it belonged to. When he realized it was mine, he tracked me down on Facebook and told me that he'd do whatever he could to get it to me. I'd thought that the camera was long gone, and I was so happy to know that I hadn't lost the footage on the memory card in the camera, not that Adidas would have cared. Not long after losing the camera, I called Dorothy and found out that they'd changed their minds about making a documentary about me. They'd talked about putting my footage on their website and tracking my progress as I hiked north, but then they bailed on that idea. My guess is that they didn't realize that it would take me so long to hike the AT. Most people usually take four to six months to complete the entire trek, but the setbacks that I'd suffered because of my stump meant that it was going to take a lot longer than six months. I didn't think it was a big deal, though. I figured that it was a major accomplishment no matter how long it took, but I think

I didn't fit into their timeline. Oh well. I was doing this for myself, not for Adidas, or for anyone else for that matter.

I got on Facebook Messenger and coordinated with Ron to have the camera mailed to me at a local hostel called Four Pines. I asked if there was anything I could do for him, if I could give him some type of reward for returning the camera to me. He joked that I could buy him a Subway sandwich if we ever met in person, but he refused to take anything else. Just minutes after discovering a box full of free food for hikers, I talked to a guy who was bending over backwards to have my camera mailed to me. As happened often while I was on the trail, I was struck by the kindness of other hikers. If I'd lost that camera in some big city somewhere, my best chance of finding it probably would have been to get on Craigslist and buy it back from the person who'd found it. But out here on the AT—on just about any trail really—I could usually count on meeting people who genuinely care about the well-being of others. The hiking community has done so much for me on my thru-hikes, but their generosity never ceases to amaze me.

After a few more days of hiking, I arrived at Glasgow and contacted High Noon. He told me that he'd found a deal on a kayak at Kmart, only $245. I told him I was about sixty-five miles south of Waynesboro. He offered to pick me up. I agreed because otherwise he would have had to have waited for me for more than a week while I hiked up there. I was really looking forward to climb in a kayak and spend ten days off my feet, paddling on the river.

He arrived with a couple ice cold IPAs, and we sat on the banks of the Maury River, drinking and chatting. He told me that he'd met Almost Triple Crowner, the woman with the service dog. He'd been at an outdoor sporting goods store where she had a rubber boat delivered. When she told the owner of the store that she intended to use the boat for kayaking on the South River, the man told her that she was making a huge mistake. She refused to listen to his explanations about why it was a bad idea, and the owner of the store became increasingly frustrated with her. After she left, she reached out to High Noon to see if he wanted to go aqua blazing with her. He told her that he already had other plans. A few days later, we saw a Facebook post from her describing how her rubber boat had been destroyed by rocks, but somehow, she got her hands on a kayak and was able to continue. More power to her.

James River Bridge in Glasgow, Virginia

Eventually we loaded my gear into his car and headed out. On the way to Waynesboro, we pulled over to make camp for the night. He pitched a tent, and I slept in his car. It wasn't the most comfortable night of sleep, but then it also wasn't the worst one I'd had over the past couple months.

The next morning, we bought our kayaks at Kmart. His car was a little four-door sedan, and after we mounted and tied the kayaks to the roof, the car looked ridiculous, like a small child wearing a hiker's backpack. We then drove to a grocery store to stock up for the ten-day trip from Waynesboro to Harpers Ferry, West Virginia. You'd think that two experienced hikers would be experts in shopping for long wilderness trips, but we bought way too much stuff. It took us forever to load everything into our kayaks, down by the river. And it took me even longer to tape the bottom of my kayak with the Gorilla Tape that I hoped would protect it from the rocks.

The beginning of my kayak adventure in Waynesboro near the Shenandoah River

I was excited to get into the water after we'd finished our preparations. It had been a while since I'd last kayaked, and I was excited for the change of pace. I knew that the muscles in my upper body were going to be exhausted when we set up camp at the end of the day, but I was looking forward to giving my amputated leg a break for a while.

I was grinning from ear to ear when we climbed into our kayaks and pushed out into the water, but my smile quickly faded. Just a few feet from shore, High Noon's kayak capsized, and all the gear he'd just loaded into the hatch compartment dumped out into the river. This wasn't exactly an auspicious start to our aqua blazing adventure.

We dragged his kayak back onto dry land, dumped out the water he'd taken on, and waded into the river to collect all the gear he'd lost. It took us an hour to pull everything out and load it back into his kayak. Then we took off again, but my excitement was muted this time. I didn't want to get my hopes up too high.

We didn't have any problems for the rest of the day. We paddled down the river for a few hours, enjoying the tranquility. Except for the signs that we occasionally saw that read, "No trespassing or camping. We have guns," our surroundings were beautiful. We kept on until night approached, when we started looking for a place to set up camp.

After some searching, we saw from a distance a sort of access tunnel to the river, where I could hang up my hammock and High Noon could pitch his tent. We ate dinner, then we settled in for the night. The muscles in my arms and my back ached, but I fell asleep quickly. The physical strain of the day had drained my body.

Early the next morning, we ate most of the fresh produce we bought in town, before climbing back into our kayaks and pushing off. As serene as the river had been the previous day, it was even more tranquil now. Except for the birdsong that fluttered in from every direction, there were few sounds to break the quiet of the early morning.

Until we came upon some rapids. As the current quickened, my adrenalin spiked. High Noon paddled out in front of me, and he entered a tricky passage of boulders and bends. If I'd been on my own, I would have walked along the shore and past the rapids with my kayak, but my ego wouldn't let me take the alternative route. (Hiking around the rapids). I studied High Noon's maneuvers carefully, knowing that I'd be traversing the same path in moments. He handled the rapids skillfully, and I was confident I could manage them as well. Wishful thinking.

In the first set of rapids, my kayak spun until it was perpendicular to the river banks, and it was pushed against a boulder that rose above the waterline. Water flooded into my compartment, wedging my kayak against the boulder and bending the plastic hull. I pushed, pulled, and twisted my kayak away from that boulder. Good thing the river was shallow. I tried tugging the kayak out of the water, but there was no way I was going to move the goddamn thing on my own. It was full of what I guessed must be several hundred pounds of water. I'd need High Noon's help to take out my gear and drag the kayak to shore.

I saw High Noon downriver, and I waved both arms in a 45-degree angle up and down—the official signal for help. He must have misinterpreted my waves because he never returned for me. I waited for him for more than an hour before I gave up and decided to try something else. I was worried that the pressure of the water might break the kayak in half against the boulder and put an end to our adventure before it even really started, so I dug the Gorilla Tape out from the hatch compartment and taped my prosthetic around my quad. I wasn't about to lose that $10,000 leg. Then I got on my butt in the water and let the current take me down the river. It was a little intimidating without the kayak to protect me from the boulders, but I managed to make my way down to High Noon's kayak. I was worried that he might have been eaten by swarms of mosquitos or carried away by a giant dragon, but he was having a great time on a sandbank, smoking pot and drinking beer.

We hiked along the river bank back to my kayak. The big bushes and the uneven terrain made the trip really difficult for me, but the hike wasn't nearly as challenging as pulling the water-logged kayak away from that boulder. We had to empty the hatch compartment, drain it, and repack everything again. This was definitely my worst ever start to a kayaking trip.

I was tired and soaked when I climbed back into my kayak and headed down the river, and I didn't feel like paddling until sunset. I asked High Noon if he minded stopping for the day so we could search for a private property where we could set up camp for the night. I think he wanted to push on, but he agreed to stop for my sake.

We wanted to get permission from whoever owned the property we were going to crash on for the night. We discovered a house on the first promising piece of land we found, but we couldn't locate the owner. I called out and peeked in the house's windows, but there were no signs of anyone. We gave up on that place and found another house, where there were a ton of people apparently having a party. I found High Noon and told him about it, and his response was to crack open another beer. He'd had several cans already, not to mention some whiskey shots, and his speech had become slurred. I thought he'd get excited by the prospect of crashing a party, but he told me that he now wanted to continue paddling while there was still daylight left. I really wasn't in the mood for navigating rapids, and he was in no condition to be on the river. He was fairly drunk, and I know he'd smoked at least one bowl. I told him that I was concerned for his safety, that people die when they mix extreme sports and alcohol, but he wouldn't listen to reason. He was going to go with or without me. I decided that we'd better stick together because I wouldn't be able to live with the guilt if something happened and I wasn't around to help him.

When we got on the river, I paddled out in front of him. He started yelling at me from behind, asking me in a slurred voice if I wanted to race him. I told him that I didn't feel like racing; he told me that was fine because his wrist was bothering him anyway. He also said he had a stress fracture in his foot because he'd hiked too many miles in a short period, and he was hoping that ten days on the river would help his body heal. I wondered if he'd gotten so drunk because he was frustrated that walking hurt his foot and paddling hurt his wrist. Maybe he was afraid he wasn't going to make it to Maine.

At some point, I looked back to make sure he was all right, and I saw him standing on a sandbar in the middle of the river, taking a leak. He could barely stand up, and he couldn't find his paddle. I searched for a few minutes before locating it under his kayak, then he tried climbing back into his cockpit, but he couldn't balance well enough to get in. Alarm bells rang in my head. This situation had become really dangerous. If he fell into the river, I probably wouldn't be able to save him. Back when I had two legs, I was an excellent swimmer, and I'd taken classes in Germany to learn how to rescue people from the water. But I was only half the swimmer I used to be. High Noon was significantly taller than I was, and he outweighed me by fifty or sixty pounds. If he tripped and fell into the water, he probably would have died. Not only would I lose a friend, but I'd have to explain to the cops why I'd let someone who was so drunk kayak down a swiftly moving river.

I told him that we should make camp on the sandbar; he said in his slurred speech that there was still daylight left and that he wanted to paddle on. I knew I had to stop him. My brain offered up a series of unlikely solutions. I could knock him out with a roundhouse kick. I could pretend to be severely ill. I could tell him I wouldn't continue on with him unless he stopped for the day. But before I could come up with a plausible plan, he was back in the kayak, and we were heading down the river again.

A few hours later, I saw a sandy cove that was populated by a bale of turtles. I told High Noon I was stopping to watch them, and I waved him over to see them. I thought this was an ideal place for setting up camp, and I hoped I could distract him long enough to get him out of the kayak and onto dry land. He paddled toward me, and I thought for a moment that I'd finally convinced him to call it a day. But before he entered the cove, he told me that there was still an hour of daylight left, and he took off down the river. I hadn't seen him drink for the past few hours, so I decided to let him go. I was angry at that point. I'd realized over the course of the day that I didn't know the guy at all.

I thought I'd gotten a good feel for his personality while we were on the AT, but I'd been sadly mistaken. I never imagined that he could be dumb enough to drink so much on the river that he'd be a danger to himself and to me, and I wasn't going to drown trying to save a drunk.

I hung my hammock and spread out my gear, so it could dry overnight. Then I ate dinner while watching the sunset. It was a beautiful evening, and it would have been nice to sit there enjoying life without a worry, but I couldn't stop my mind from imagining dark thoughts. I was sincerely afraid that I'd find his bloated body floating face down in the river the next day, and I had a really hard time falling asleep that night.

I woke up the next morning before dawn to look for High Noon. I paddled slowly, hoping I wouldn't see his overturned kayak around every bend. About ten or fifteen minutes after I set out, I saw his kayak resting on the bank of a portion of the river that passed under a bridge. I didn't see him yet, but I was pretty sure at that point that he was fine. I breathed a sigh of relief.

Eventually I found High Noon passed out on a boulder under the bridge. I could only imagine how uncomfortable his night must have been, not that he'd noticed. His body was obviously numb to the discomfort. I suppose that's the one benefit of being obnoxiously drunk: it's a surefire cure for insomnia. You can sleep like a baby on a boulder under a busy automobile bridge.

I pulled my kayak up next to his and climbed out of the cockpit. He was passed out cold, and it took some doing to wake him up. He apologized profusely for getting so drunk. I told him I didn't mind, but the truth was that I was still upset. This was only our second full day on the river, and I was having to bring my partner back from the dead. I didn't like the direction this adventure was heading.

We drank some coffee, then we climbed into our kayaks and headed down the river. High Noon wasn't nearly as spirited as he'd been the day before, and he trailed well behind me. Every half hour or so, I stopped to let him catch up.

Late in the afternoon, we arrived at our first dam. Dams are definitely the least enjoyable part of aqua blazing, or maybe the second least after drunken paddling buddies. You have to remove your gear from your kayak and carry it all down in multiple trips. Then you have to come back for the kayak, which weighs as much as two or three backpacks. Suffice it to say, I wasn't looking forward to our next dam.

Before we could re-enter the river on the other side of the dam, High Noon decided that he couldn't go on. His wrist was more injured than he realized, and he was in too much pain to continue paddling. He told me that he wanted to hitchhike back to Waynesboro to get his car, and he wanted me to wait for him, so he could give me a ride over the dam the next morning. He left, then I got my gear out of the hatch compartment, so it could dry out.

---

*"If the plan doesn't work,
change the plan, but never the goal."*
~ Unknown

When I opened up the waterproof bag that contained my cell, I discovered that water had seeped into the bag, and my phone was completely ruined, dead as a doornail.

Forty minutes later, a car approached me in the parking lot, and a woman rolled down her window and asked if I was the Bionic Woman. I pointed at my prosthetic leg and smiled. She introduced herself as Lynn and said that High Noon had sent her to tell me that he was at a nearby gas station. She'd volunteered to give him a ride to

Waynesboro and then to pick me up and take me to her house. And this wasn't a quick trip around the block. The round-trip drive would take her several hours. More trail magic!

When she arrived later that afternoon, she was accompanied by the three young grandchildren she was raising for her daughter. As she drove me to her house, the kids peppered me with questions, mostly about my leg. Did it hurt when they cut it off? Did I miss it? Was it hard learning to walk on a "fake" leg? I answered all their questions with a grin. Their excitement was catching.

I had a lovely dinner with the family, and it felt wonderful to sleep on an air-mattress that night. After spending so much of the previous night worrying about High Noon, I slept like a rock.

We ate a quick breakfast at her house before we hopped into her car to head back down to the river. Because I was on my own now, I decided that it would be best to skip all those damn dams, so she drove me down to Gooney Creek, about thirty miles downriver from where I'd met her the previous day. To show my gratitude for the rides to and from the river and for the use of her home, I offered to give her grandson my kayak when I arrived at Harpers Ferry. The boy grinned like a jack-o-lantern.

Back on the river, I enjoyed the solitude of solo paddling. Now that I didn't have to worry about High Noon drowning, I wasn't stressed. And I liked being able to decide when and where to stop. One of the best parts of traveling alone is that you don't have to worry about synchronizing your desires with those of your travel partner. It's nice to have someone to talk to while you're out in the middle of nowhere, but sometimes the compromises aren't worth the conversation.

Later that morning while I was paddling in the sun, I came across several kids who were doing back flips into the river from a rock that was about forty feet above the water. Before my accident, I probably would have climbed up on that rock and joined them in their fun, but that didn't seem like a good idea now. I'd likely damage my prosthetic if I jumped in from that height, so that wasn't an option. It also wouldn't be a good idea to hop around on one leg forty feet above the river, so that was off the table as well. It wasn't a big deal in the end, but I did feel some nostalgia for the days when I had fewer physical limitations. I was on this journey both to recover my strength and to prove to myself that there was so much that I could still do in spite of my disability, but there were times like now when I was forced to accept that there were things I just couldn't do any more.

Later that day, I came to the final dam I'd have to cross. I'd skipped most of the dams, which meant that the hardest part of the trip down the river was behind me, but I still had this one monster to deal with. I had to take eight half-mile trips back and forth from one side of the dam to the other to transfer all my gear. It was torture, but at least this was the last time I'd have to do it. I was really happy that Lynn had driven me past all those dams.

I settled into a comforting routine over the next week. I woke up early, spent most of the day floating and paddling, and then went to bed shortly after sunset. It was a peaceful time, full of hours of reflection and relaxation. I enjoyed every minute of it, but as I approached my destination, my feet began to itch for a return to the trail. Now that my legs were well rested, it was time to start abusing them again.

I arrived at Watermelon Park nine days after leaving Waynesboro. At a camping goods store, I met a woman who let me camp outside for free and allowed me to use her phone to call my friend Diane to ask her to send me the backup phone I'd left in her care. It's funny how much I missed my cell. I felt so detached from my friends, and I was looking forward to reconnecting with them via Facebook.

One of those Facebook friends was a woman named Judy, who'd offered to pick me up at Harpers Ferry. She'd read an article about my walk on the AT, and she reached out to me and offered me a ride. I wasn't technically on the trail, but she's definitely a trail angel in my book.

I had a nice muffin and some coffee at the camping goods store the next morning, then I departed Watermelon Park for Harpers Ferry. It was a quick two-hour trip, and I enjoyed every minute of it because I didn't know when I'd next have an opportunity to spend so much time floating down a river. Near the dam at Harpers Ferry, I came upon a party of twenty or so people. I didn't know what they were celebrating, but they invited me to join them. They were grilling juicy steaks and fat pork chops, and they had bowl after bowl of side dishes. Best of all, they had Jägermeister! It was a blast, but I couldn't stay long. Judy was expecting my call, so I borrowed a phone from a guy at the party, and I gave her a ring to let her know that I was ready to be picked up, whenever she was ready to get me.

When she arrived, Judy helped load my gear into her trunk and secure my kayak to the roof of her car, then she drove me to her house. She was such a gracious host, and she bent over backwards to make me comfortable. In fact, after I got settled into her place on my first night, she spoiled me with dinner at a fancy restaurant. And the next day, she gave me her iPod and helped me download a bunch of audiobooks and music from her computer in order to make my long days on the AT a little more pleasant. In the coming weeks, I'd fall in love with some of the stories on those audiobooks. Born to Run by Christopher McDougall was my favorite, but Wild by Cheryl Strayed was a close second. I also really enjoyed A Walk in the Woods by Bill Bryson, as well as a handful of other titles by thru-hikers on the AT. It was an interesting experience to listen to stories about the places I was visiting. The books were like my own personal guided tours.

That same day, Lynn came to Judy's house to pick up the kayak I promised to give her grandson. She was happy to receive it; I was happy to give it a good home.

Lynn's grandson in the kayak I gave him

I spent four relaxing days at Judy's house before my cell phone arrived. Toward the end of my stay, I started looking for a rental car to drive to Maine. Given the setbacks I'd experienced during the first phase of my hike, it was clear that it would take me far longer to finish the AT than I anticipated. At my current pace, I'd end up in the mountains of Maine in the middle of winter, and I knew I wouldn't be able to finish the last leg of my hike if I had to trek through snow. Even if I still had both of my legs, I didn't have the equipment I'd need to hike in winter conditions. A winter sleeping bag, snow boots, warm clothes—I didn't have anything. Besides that, Mount Katahdin, the last section of the AT, shuts down in early October, so there was no way I could hike on as a north bounder. I decided that I had to do a flip-flop thru-hike, which meant that I was going to drive to Maine now while conditions were good, and from there I'd hike south to where I'd left the trail in Glasgow. This wasn't exactly how I imagined my hike would go, but I didn't mind the change of plans. The AT wasn't going anywhere, and I didn't have any pressing plans after I finished my hike. There was nowhere I needed to be. I'd finish when I finished.

As soon as my backup phone arrived at Judy's house, I started making plans to head north. I contacted a Couchsurfing host in Connecticut, halfway to Maine. I also found a good deal on a tiny rental car. Before I headed north, Judy drove me to the Appalachian Trail Conservancy, the midway point of the trail, where they take photos to keep track of how many people hike the AT every year.

The halfway point at the Appalachian Trail Conservancy
in Harpers Ferry, West Virginia

Taking a photo in front of the AT Conservancy sign was symbolically important to me. I technically wasn't halfway done because I'd have to hike from Maine to Glasgow, which was south of the midway point, but then I wasn't far from being half finished. There were times in the earliest stages of the hike when I doubted that I'd be able to complete the hike. To my knowledge, only one person had ever completed the AT on a prosthetic, and for good reason. It's damn hard! Even under the best of circumstances, the trail takes a lot out of you, which is why only twenty to twenty five percent of the people who decide to thru-hike the AT actually complete it. The prosthetic makes it that much more difficult, especially when you're hiking only fourteen short months after getting your leg amputated. But here I was, close to half done. I could do this. I could finish what I'd started. I would finish. I had no doubt now.

11

MISERY IN MAINE

East Coast toll roads suck. That's what I discovered as I drove up to Mount Katahdin, Maine. I cringed every time I had to stop and hand over my money at a tollbooth. I didn't have much cash to spare, and every dollar I spent at a tollbooth was a dollar I didn't have to spend on resupplying my food stock. I'd have to cut out everything that wasn't a necessity. I definitely didn't have money in my budget for beer any more. So much for a nice frosty IPA after a tough day on the trail.

I was driving a little Fiat Punto, and I was excited to put it to the test on the interstate. I stepped on the gas, and that little car really took off…right past a cop car sitting on the shoulder of the road. I shook my head in frustration. I definitely hadn't budgeted for a speeding ticket. Anytime I climb into or onto anything with wheels and a motor, I end up going faster than the posted speed limit.

When he walked up to my window and asked me if I knew why he'd pulled me over, I made a joke about driving on the German Autobahn, which doesn't have a speed limit. He didn't look amused, so I just closed my mouth and handed over my German driver's license and the rental car registration. While he ran my name through his system, I sat there thinking back on the other times I'd been pulled over while driving in the US. The most interesting story happened back in 2010, while I was riding my motorcycle through Nevada on my way to Alaska. When the cop pulled me over, I took off my helmet in the hope that he might take pity on a pretty girl. But it wasn't my face that got me out of a ticket that time; it was my German accent. It turned out that he had some German heritage, and we talked about Germany for quite a while. Eventually he smiled, told me to slow down a little, and sent me on my way. Not long after I left, I drove through a small town in search of some Kevlar tape to protect my gear from my muffler, which was overheating. I walked into a hardware store and saw the same cop who'd pulled me over just a couple hours earlier. He asked what I was looking for, and I told him about the tape. The store didn't carry any, but the cop said he had some. He told me to stick around for twenty minutes and he'd return. True to his word, he came back with a roll of Kevlar tape from his toolbox. He gave it to me for free, and he even mounted it onto my motorcycle. First, he let me out of a speeding ticket, then he gave me a free roll of Kevlar tape. Best police officer ever!

The cop who pulled me over on my way to Maine returned about half an hour after walking away with my German driver's license. He had a hard time locating me in his system, and I got away with a warning. That was really lucky for me because I'd missed a court hearing in Colorado when I was in Germany visiting my family. If he'd figured that out, I might have ended up in jail. And that would have ended my AT hike.

Afraid of being pulled over again, I drove like an old woman to the home of my Couchsurfing host in Bridgeport, Connecticut. I arrived somewhat late in the evening, but my hosts were incredibly accommodating. As soon as I dropped my gear in their spare bedroom, they brought out the cold beer. Thank God for the kindness of strangers! We sat in the living room for several hours exchanging stories about places we'd visited and people we'd met. Conversations like those are one of the best parts of traveling. We might have gone on talking until the wee hours, but I really needed some sleep, so I excused myself and crashed for the night.

I woke up the next morning and had breakfast with my host. After we finished, I thanked them for their generosity and got back on the road.

I drove straight to Bangor, Maine, where I found another Couch-surfing host, a woman named Rachel. I dropped off my gear at her place, then we headed to the home of Stephen King, who had been my favorite author when I was a teenager. He lives near downtown Bangor, and his red mansion reminded me of the hotel from his book: *The Shining*. I was glad I had an opportunity to see it.

Stephen King's house in Bangor, Maine

Most people who hike the AT from south to north ascend Mount Katahdin, then turn around and descend the mountain, ending their hike at the bottom of the south face. Because I was doing a flip-flop hike, I planned to ascend the north face of Katahdin and descend the south face. The day after my arrival was Rachel's day off, and she offered to drive me to the base of the north face. Like so many other people I met on the trail, she went out of her way to help me. She left me with many kind words when we said our goodbyes.

At the ranger station at the base of the north face, I had to convince the ranger that I'd reserved a campsite. I hadn't of course, but he didn't need to know that. When it was time to set up my camp that night, I introduced myself to a family and asked if they minded if I hung my hammock in some trees near their site. They said they were happy to have me, and they even invited me to eat some of their tasty barbecue. And when the ranger checked on us before we went to sleep, he found me cheerfully mingling with the family.

I got started on my hike up Katahdin the next morning. Before Rachel dropped me off, she took me to a camp store south of the mountain, and I left some of my gear there, including my rain poncho. The weather had been perfect for the past few days, the temperature creeping up into the 80s by late afternoon. All I had with me was some food, a sleeping bag, and my hammock. I was travelling light because I didn't expect the hike to be difficult. I was also travelling without a map because I was trying to be as frugal as possible. I didn't want to spend the $10, and I thought I could figure out the route without guidance.

I realized my error when I reached a summit later that day. I thought I'd climbed to Baxter Peak, but I met a couple named Carl and Julie who informed me that I'd reached Pamola Peak. I felt like a fool, but it wasn't a big deal. I could just find the trail to Baxter and climb it the next day.

"The struggle you're in today is developing the strength you need for tomorrow."
~ ROBERT TEW

Carl and Julie offered to help me descend to the midway station, and I gratefully accepted. As we made our way down the narrow trail, I realized that I was no longer on a hiking excursion. This was more like a mountaineering trip, minus the ropes and carabiners. I still wasn't all that concerned, though. The weather was decent, and my spirits were high.

On Pamola Peak instead of Baxter Peak

We arrived at the midway station hut just before dark. They offered to hike up to Baxter Peak from the south side with me the next morning, but I told them I'd be fine on my own. So, Carl and Julie headed back to the same campground I'd started at that morning. I still thought this was no big deal.

My leg was a little sore the next morning after the previous day's hike, and it took me a while to get moving. By the time I left the hut, the sky was overcast, and the temperature had dropped to the low 70s. But I still wasn't worried. Having just crossed the halfway point of my AT hike, I was full of optimism.

On my way back to the midway station

It wasn't long before I was ascending a steep rockface on my way up to Baxter Peak. I had to pull myself up hand over hand, and my sore stump wasn't doing me any favors. A light drizzle started to fall, making the rocks slippery under my trail runners. I moved very slowly so I wouldn't fall and hurt myself. As if the rain wasn't bad enough, a thick fog rolled in and blanketed the mountain, drastically reducing visibility. The final couple miles to the peak were hairy, but I pushed on. About half an hour from the top, I ran into a couple who were descending from the peak. I wanted to take some photos near the sign that marked the highest point of Katahdin, and I obviously couldn't do it myself.

After a little pleading, I convinced them to return to the peak with me, so they could photograph me. We finished the last mile together, and they took my pictures. They were both concerned about the weather, and they offered to hike with me back from where I started out that morning. I refused their generous offer, though. The temperature was in the 60s, which wasn't so bad. I was convinced that I could make it down to the bottom of Baxter, and I insisted on hiking every inch of the trail. My optimism and determination are usually sources of strength for me, but in this case, they damn near got me killed.

The highest point of Mt. Katahdin (also known as Baxter Peak)

Shortly after saying goodbye to the couple, it started raining really hard, then the wind blew, then it started to howl. Moderate gusts quickly became eighty-mile-per-hour blasts that seemed to want to throw me off the side of the mountain. It was so powerful that it knocked me to the ground three times, and more than once I nearly plummeted down a rocky cliff. This was serious. Less than an hour before, I was grinning and hamming it up for the camera, but now I was fighting for my life. If I were to have a fall similar to the one that had nearly killed me in Utah, there would be no way I could get off that mountain. No helicopter would have been able to land in those conditions. I needed to do everything I could to protect myself.

I stumbled around for a few minutes until I found a crevasse, an open crack to hunker down and ride out the storm. I pulled out my sleeping bag and crawled inside.

I thought I was safe, but the cold started gnawing at my bones. Stage one of hypothermia was setting in. My body started shivering uncontrollably and my heart rate quickened. During my training as an EMT and paramedic, I'd learned about the three stages of hypothermia, and I knew that if stage three set in, I'd become dangerously disoriented. In the final stage of hypothermia, I'd likely rip off all my clothes in an act of "paradoxical undressing," and my body would freeze solid in minutes. Back in 2006 when I was a ski instructor in Steamboat Springs, CO, I remember the story of some teenage-kids skiing out of bounds, who got caught in a blizzard. They ended up in stage three hypothermia, frozen solid with naked upper bodies.

I realized that I couldn't leave, but I also couldn't stay there. I had to do something quick.

By some miracle, my cell phone had reception. For the first time in my life, I called 911. I was able to give a detailed description of my location, although I wasn't sure if anyone would be able to find me. The fog was so dense that I could barely see my hand on my outstretched arm. When I hung up, adrenalin was rushing through my body, but I stayed calm and thought back on my paramedic training. I searched my backpack for anything that could insulate my body, but I'd been traveling light and I didn't have much in there. I also ate all the food in my pack because my body was burning so many calories by shivering to stay warm. I was munching on some food when I remembered that I hadn't told the emergency responder about a sign I'd recently passed. I still had cell reception, so I called 911 a second time. The responder assured me that help was on its way, and she comforted me for a few minutes before my cell phone battery died.

The hours that followed were miserable. My body shaking severely, I tried to move as much as possible to keep my blood circulating, but I was in a small crevasse, and I couldn't move much. The shivering wasn't fun, but I knew that as long as I was still shaking, I was in good shape. You're in trouble when your body stops shivering and you start to get really sleepy.

Two or three hours after my call for help, the sound of a high-pitched whistle caught my attention. At first, I thought it was just the wind, but then I recognized structure in the sound. There was someone out there, someone looking for me. While I'd been waiting to be rescued, I'd taken out my emergency whistle from my backpack. I put it to my lips, took in a lungful of air, and tried to blow, but my lips were frozen, and I couldn't make much sound. I rubbed my lips and blew again. My whistle shrieked this time. Another whistle came in reply moments later. We whistled back and forth until I could see the outline of a figure through the fog. I waved my hand until he saw me. He bent down and introduced himself. Then he grilled me with questions meant to test my lucidity. Did I remember calling 911? Did I know what day it was? Did I know where I was? My answers reassured him that I wasn't in stage three hypothermia, but that didn't mean I was out of the woods yet. He had some energy bars, and he asked me to sit up and eat. I'd already eaten everything in my pack after crawling into my sleeping bag, but all that energy had been quickly converted into warmth by way of shivering. My body was stiff from the cold and from immobility, so he had to help me sit up. I wasn't at all hungry, but I forced myself to eat those bars. They'd be vital for getting off that mountain.

While I ate, we turned our attention to my wet clothes. I had to get them off, even if it meant exposing my bare body to the elements. The thought of the frigid wind and rain biting at my naked skin made it difficult for me to stand up, but the ranger was very encouraging. He helped me up and looked away as I stripped off my soaked clothing. He'd brought rain gear with him, and I pulled everything on as quickly as my shivering body would permit. Once I was dressed, he gave me a woolen cap to prevent my body heat from escaping through my bare head. Hands, feet, and head—that's where a freezing body loses most of its warmth. I could no longer feel my hands, and my toes were frozen in my Adidas trail runners. Those shoes are supposed to be waterproof, but after a thousand miles of hiking, they weren't exactly in pristine condition.

Besides being as stiff as a popsicle, I'd also pulled a muscle in my good leg. It wasn't going to be easy descending the mountain. As we started moving, we were completely exposed to the wind again. The ranger walked in front of me, and I held on to his backpack, thinking that the wind wouldn't blow us both down. But it flung us to the ground like ragdolls. We tried to stand, but the wind was just too powerful. We decided to crawl to minimize the chances that the furious wind would blow us off the mountain. While still above the tree line, we had to use some technical maneuvers to descend some craggy sections. When we encountered gaps, we made our way down by pushing our backs against the boulders and walking our bodies to the bottom. At some point during our climb down, I strained that muscle in my good leg even more, making everything way more difficult. Now I had a bad limp to go with my hypothermia.

It took us more than three hours to get below the tree line, where we finally had some protection from the wind. We were met by another ranger. He greeted us with hot drinks and food. It felt like I was getting first-class service from some sort of "meals on boots" service. I got some more food in my belly, then we continued down to the base of the mountain. A huge fire awaited me inside the ranger station. It was about 1 a.m. when I walked into the hut and sat near those beautiful flames. When you're as cold as I was, the concept of heat seems so foreign that it's almost unimaginable. There was a time when I wasn't sure I'd ever know the comfort of warmth again and sitting there defrosting my frozen body was an indescribable pleasure. I'll probably never enjoy a fire more than I enjoyed that one. And I'll likely never drink hot chocolate that will taste better than the stuff I had that night. There's nothing like privation to make you appreciate the small stuff that you usually take for granted.

Once I was completely thawed, the rangers showed me outside to a lean-to, where they'd prepared a place for me to sleep. The Therm-a-Rest that lay on the ground was calling my name. My body had expended tremendous amounts of energy to keep itself alive, and it was screaming for rest. I was grateful I didn't have to set up my hammock, and I was practically asleep before my head hit that mat.

I woke up the next morning and went into the ranger's office, expecting to get chewed out for letting myself get trapped in such dangerous conditions. I also thought I was going to get hit with a huge bill for my rescue. To my surprise, the chief ranger wasn't at all upset. He said he was glad I'd called 911 before I was seriously injured. He told me horror stories about rescuing day climbers who'd tried to tackle Baxter Peak in flip flops and without any food or water. Compared to some of those rescues, saving me was a day in the park for him. It turns out that he was an expert hiker who'd finished the PCT, the AT, and the CDT. He was in such good shape that it had only taken him two and a half hours to reach me. I got lucky that my rescuer was such an exceptional athlete and a reasonable man.

I made it down the mountain the next day, but I didn't make it unscathed. I had mild frostbite on my fingers and toes. I wasn't happy with yet another setback, but all things considered, I was lucky I'd escaped with such minor injuries. For those who are counting, like a cat with nine lives, I'm on my second last life.

No, actually, by now I'm on my LAST life! Back in 2002, I visited my uncle in Kitimat, Canada, for the first time. His son and a friend drove with me to a river where we jumped off a 50-foot bridge. When I jumped and came out of the water, I took another breath, but a strong current suddenly pulled me back down under.

Back in Germany, I was a rescue swimmer, and I learned that people get killed when they start to panic or fight the current, so I stayed calm and tried to relax. That training was why I came back up to the surface and made it back to shore safely. Yes, for those counting, I am on my last life.

---

*"No matter how much it hurts now,
one day you will look back and realize
it changed your life for the better."*
~ Unknown

That day on the AT I decided that it was best not to push my luck, so I checked into a tiny attic room at a hostel called the Appalachian Trail Lodge in Millinocket. I wanted to make sure my body was completely healed before I started beating it up on the trail again. If I got an infection in my toes, I risked losing parts of my good leg.

I checked in, crawled into bed, and slept. Then I slept some more. When the woman who owned the hostel didn't hear from me for twenty-four hours, she knocked on my door, worried if I was still alive. She brought some beverages for me and told me that she owned a breakfast joint in town. She offered to serve me a meal in her restaurant.

Food was just what I needed after burning so many calories on Katahdin.

I stayed in Millinocket for three days. I would have liked to have spent another day recuperating, but I didn't have much cash to spare. I had a hundred-mile stretch of wilderness coming up, and I needed the money for groceries. My budget was getting tighter by the day, and I had to mind every cent.

The part of the trail that I was about to undertake, which ran from Katahdin to Monson, was notoriously difficult. In fact, it poses such a risk to hikers that the Maine Appalachian Trail Club has posted a sign that says:

"There are no places to obtain supplies or get help until Abol Bridge 100 miles north. Do not attempt this section unless you have a minimum of 10 days of supplies and are fully equipped. This is the longest wilderness section of the entire AT and its difficulty should not be underestimated. Good hiking!"

The so-called Hundred-Mile Wilderness is one of the most gorgeous parts of the AT, but it's also ridiculously challenging. Danger lurks everywhere, especially for the unprepared hiker. You have to ford several rivers that are fed by snowmelt, and each one of them can easily kill a hiker toting around a backpack full of more than a week of supplies. A slip in one of those rivers can lead to a lungful of frigid water. Falls are also a serious threat. The Hundred-Mile Wilderness is home to craggy mountains that can be treacherous. More than one hiker has died from a head injury caused by a fall. And as I'd just learned on Katahdin, the weather could quickly turn deadly. I'd been smart enough to avoid hiking through this section of the AT during winter, but that didn't mean that I couldn't be caught in a nasty storm that could send the temperature plummeting. Death by hypothermia is a very real threat on this part of the trail.

The woman who owns the hostel provides rides for hikers. After dropping off a load of hikers who were heading north to fight the mountain that had nearly cost me my life, the van stopped at the camp store, so I could pick up the rest of my supplies. The owner wanted to charge me more for the extra three days of storage, but when I told him about my adventure on Katahdin, he forgave my debt. People who do business with hikers on a regular basis are sensitive to the struggles of their customers, and a tale of a harrowing experience on the trail can soften hearts.

I got back on the trail that day, loaded down with ten to twelve days of supplies. I was still sore from my brush with death on Katahdin, and it was difficult to get my body moving. My toes and my fingers were still numb, but they didn't slow me down much. My biggest issue was my good leg, which was still stiff from the three hours I spent lying on the rocky ground buried in my sleeping bag. I had to use my hiking poles to walk, and even then, it was slow going. I reminded myself over and over again that the things that don't kill me make me stronger.

I only hiked a few miles that day. I would have liked to have pushed on before stopping for the day, but my body needed the rest. It was still early afternoon when I found a nice place next to a serene lake to set up camp. I hung my hammock between two trees, climbed in, and fell asleep immediately. That was probably the earliest I turned in the whole time I was on the trail.

I slept more than sixteen hours that day and that night, and I got up early, so I could make up for lost time. My body was a little less sore after more than half a day of sleep. I expected smooth sailing that day, but then came the clouds of black flies. Swarms of them followed me everywhere I went. They weren't biting flies, but they were still a nuisance. They were drawn to my eyes, my ears, and my nostrils, and no amount of waving and swiping could drive them off. They seemed hell-bent on finding a way to crawl into my head.

Distracted by the legions of flying kamikazes, I made a wrong turn on the trail, and before I knew it, I was climbing over felled trees and massive boulders. I eventually realized that I'd wandered off the AT. It took me about two hours to retrace my steps and find the place I'd made a wrong turn.

I was a mess by the time I got back on the trail. Those damn flies followed me the whole way, and both my stump and my good leg were killing me. I'd wasted four hours wandering the backcountry, and I'd have to make up for lost time before the day ended. I only had enough food in my pack to last me a week and a half. I pushed on, limping and swatting, cursing and grimacing. A glance at my trail guide told me that there was a service road a couple miles from where I'd gotten lost. I was so frustrated with the AT.

At that point I told myself if a pink Cadillac showed up with a cold six-pack of IPA, I was quitting. I was going to drink those beers until I was drunk and hitch a ride in that Cadillac to the nearest town. Then I'd get back to a life without flies and bitter wind and pain that pushed my mind past the point of endurance. What the hell was I doing out here? My body was already back to the strength, what I was hoping to accomplish. I could walk away now, and I would have achieved my goal of walking my way to recovery. What was I trying to prove?

But I knew that there was no pink Cadillac coming with frosty beer. And I wasn't leaving the trail. No matter how much my mind fantasized about soft beds and pain-free days, there was no way I could possibly quit. I'd come too far to give up. I'd endured too much agony to walk away before crossing the finish line. I thought about all the people I'd met on the trail who'd done such amazing things to help me achieve my goal. I couldn't let them down. I couldn't live with myself if I walked away before finishing the last of those 2,200 miles. I was going to push on until I was done.

Before arriving at the service road, I decided that I needed to do something about the pain in my stump, my toes, my fingers, my back, my hip — there weren't many parts of my body that didn't burn or throb. I sat down and dug out the heavy-duty pain meds from my backpack. I knew there would be side effects, including constipation and stomach cramps, but I had to manage the pain. It was wearing down my will and threatening to spoil my plans. Sometimes you have to give in to push on.

I didn't find that pink Cadillac when I reached the service road, but I did run into a couple thru-hikers from Minnesota. They were walking with a dachshund, a German breed. That little guy had walked on his stubby legs all the way from Georgia to the Hundred-Mile Wilderness. I took it as a sign. If that tiny German doggie could complete the AT, this German-American chick could do it as well. I needed to get my act together and stop whining. Negativity was doing me no favors. I needed to purge pessimism from my system, so I could finish this difficult stretch of the trail.

"Don't quit. Suffer now and live the rest of your life as a champion."
~ Muhammad Ali

A Couple with a Dachshund in the Hundred-Mile Wilderness

Just a few miles after I met that couple and their dachshund, I came across two other hikers who were traveling the Hundred-Mile Wilderness together. One was called Sunflower, and the other was called Tall Legs. I'd met Sunflower at the hostel in Millinocket. She'd earned her name when she gave a sunflower to a trail angel who'd helped her. She'd been looking for a hiking partner, but I was recuperating when she left. I was glad she'd found a buddy in Tall Legs.

We decided to hike together to a nearby beach. It was gorgeous, so we went for a swim. Being a European chick by birth, I had no problem stripping off my clothes and jumping into the water in my birthday suit. Sunflower joined me, but Tall Legs was too shy to take his clothes off in front of us. Instead, he enjoyed the view and soaked his feet in the water.

When we were done, we made a campfire to warm ourselves. We sat, chatted, and enjoyed a meal together. I marveled at the change in my mood from the beginning of the day to the end. Not half a day earlier, I'd been flirting with the idea of quitting. But here I was sharing a relaxing night with two hikers who helped me turn a miserable day around. One of my worst days on the trail had become something pleasant and uplifting. These were just the people I needed to run into to recharge my emotional battery.

Relaxing at a beach, camping spot in the Hundred-Mile Wilderness

The three of us hiked together the next day. We made it to the halfway point of the Hundred-Mile Wilderness, where the staff from the hostel in Millinocket dropped off resupply boxes for hikers. While Sunflower and Tall Legs were looking for their boxes, I met a thru-hiker named Ginger. Unlike most AT hikers, she'd started in Maine and was working her way south. I was impressed that she'd spent her first days on the trail hiking two of the hardest sections.

Ginger had been going through a divorce when she decided to hike the AT as a way of turning a new page on her life. After she was done, she intended to write a book about her experiences on the trail. But when I saw what she was transferring from her box to her backpack, I wondered if she'd be able to make it to the end. She was clearly new to distance hiking. She hadn't yet learned that every ounce counts. She had an electric toothbrush with spare batteries, a douche, cosmetics, and all sorts of knickknacks that quickly make a backpack unbearably heavy. We helped her jettison some of the extra weight. She left the toothbrush, the douche, and some of the knickknacks in her supply box, which the hostel owner would pick up on her next run. She gave some of her extra food to Sunflower, Tall Legs, and me. And she gifted me a bottle of body lotion for my stump. It was a win-win for everyone. We asked Ginger to join us on our hike through the second half of the Hundred-Mile Wilderness. She said she was delighted to have the company. The four of us left shortly after we loaded our supplies into our packs.

We hiked some tough terrain that day, including a couple quick-moving rivers. I was happy to be traveling with this little band, but I was especially grateful for Tall Legs' presence. He used those long legs to help me to cross the rivers safely. Without him, my day would have been far more taxing.

I typically struggled to keep up with able-bodied hikers, but my new hiking companions stopped often to eat snacks. My metabolism is exceptionally slow, and I don't burn as many calories as other hikers, which meant that I didn't need to stop as often as the others to eat. Our pace worked out well.

Resupply spot in the Hundred-Mile Wilderness

At the end of that day, we arrived at a campsite where we met some other hikers who'd already built a campfire. One of them was a guy called Celtic, and he wore a hiking kilt that looked a lot like my own kilt. He was hiking with his wife, Tiny Feet. I was shocked when I looked down at her belly and saw that she was several months pregnant. People were always telling me how tough I was for hiking on one leg, but I had nothing on Tiny Feet. I could only imagine how difficult it must be to hike the AT with another person in your belly. The extra weight, the morning sickness, the nutritional demands—none of that was an easy burden to bear. She impressed the hell out of me.

We sat down and got to telling stories about ourselves. I found out that the couple lived in Manhattan. She was a school teacher, and he was the owner of an outdoor sporting company that offered hiking and kayak sightseeing trips to tourists in NYC. Like many hikers on the AT, they lived for adventures like the one we were all sharing.

Celtic and Tiny Feet

Their stories about their life in Manhattan stirred up a lot of memories about an experience I had in the Big Apple back in 2003, when I was cycling from Key West to New York City. While I was riding through New Jersey, I met a couple outside a café, and they took an interest in me. They asked me where I was headed; I told them NYC. They said I was crazy for riding into the big city all by myself. That wasn't the first time I'd heard something along those lines, some warning meant to deter me from cycling into New York City unaccompanied. I was in my late twenties at the time, I was athletic, and I'd been riding my bike all across North America for months. But based on the replies I got from people when I told them my plans to visit NYC, you'd think I was a seven-year-old girl telling people about my plans to visit the den of cannibals.

The couple invited me to stay in a guest room at their home for the night. Their house was incredible. It wasn't very old by European standards, but it was ancient for America. Every step evoked a creak, and each time a door opened, hinges groaned. It was as if the house were speaking.

They were so concerned for my safety that they contacted a friend in Manhattan. The guy had an empty apartment in downtown Riverside, just a few blocks from Central Park. He offered me full use of his place for as long as I wanted it. I jumped at the chance. I thought these people were ridiculous to be so worried about my safety, but if they wanted to arrange a free stay at a downtown Manhattan apartment, I wasn't going to talk them out of it.

On my way to the Big Apple in 2003

When I arrived at the apartment lobby later that day, the doorman handed me a spare key and pointed me to the right elevator. I went up and let myself into a beautiful apartment that I didn't have to pay a cent to stay in.

The owner emailed the next day to make sure I was completely comfortable. He also asked me if I liked Broadway shows. Of course, I like Broadway shows, I told him. Who doesn't? He sent me his password for his theater club and told me to print out tickets for as many shows as I wanted to see. Because he offered, I invited a gay couple I'd met on Couchsurfing.com to a show whose main act featured a gay couple. We had a blast together.

At a Broadway show in 2003

I befriended a bicycle messenger during my stay. I rode behind him a couple times while he delivered messages, and I was shocked by how crazy he was. He rode like a madman, and it always seemed like he was just seconds away from being hit by a car.

One day we got to talking about our pasts, and I told him that I'd been a professional boxer and a kickboxer back in Europe. He told me that he was a boxer as well, and he was competing ones in the "Golden Gloves" competition in NYC. He invited me to go with him to the Bronx gym where he trained.

The gym oozed pure testosterone. I almost expected to see Sylvester Stallone in the Movie "Rocky" hitting the speed bag or to hear "The Eye of the Tiger" playing on a radio.

"Never wait for a perfect moment,
just take a moment and make it perfect."
~ Unknown

I probably should have just kept my mouth shut and just watched my friend train, but I couldn't resist throwing out a challenge to the young guys in there.

"I won the kickboxing world championship in Copenhagen in '98. Who wants to spar with me?"

All the guys in my weight class (welterweight) turned away. Only a single heavyweight took me up on my offer.

"I'm down," he said.

Seeing how big he was, I regretted the challenge, but my ego wouldn't let me back down. He gave me some worn-out gloves, and we headed into the ring. I asked him not to punch me into my teeth because I didn't have a mouth guard. He nodded, we touched gloves and started sparring. Everybody ignored us for the first couple rounds. We had a couple onlookers after the third or fourth round. But by the sixth round, the whole gym was standing around the ring, and everyone was cheering me on because I was putting up a good fight against a guy who was double my weight. I think I probably changed some minds about the meaning of "hitting like a girl."

Afterwards, the bicycle messenger and I went to an Irish pub to celebrate the one-year anniversary of the start of my bicycle tour through North America. We had a couple beers, then I burned my return airline ticket from Mexico City to Berlin. I had a one-year stand-by return flight, but here I was in a pub in New York City. This wasn't at all where I expected to be when I began my trip. But somehow, I always seemed to be in the right place at the right time, and that two-year bicycle journey was one of the best times of my life.

After spending two months at that Manhattan apartment, I decided to put my chef skills to work. I cooked a first-class meal of Schnitzel and Spätzle for the owner of the apartment and his wife and for the New Jersey couple who'd arranged for me to stay there. I also invited my bicycle messenger friend. They raved about my tasty German cooking.

Burning my return airline ticket from Mexico City to Berlin in an Irish pub in NYC

My stories about my New York City adventure must have inspired Celtic and Tiny Feet because they invited me to stay a night or two at their place in Manhattan. Apparently, there was a train station that stopped close to the AT. If I wanted to visit NYC, it would only take an hour to get downtown. Woohoo! Eight days after getting frostbite on my fingers and toes on Katahdin—I was heading back to the Big Apple!

The next day, Ginger, Sunflower, Tall Legs, and I followed a side trail to a lean-to shelter to cook lunch. After eating, Sunflower headed back to the trail before the rest of us. She was a short distance in front of me, and I heard her stop to ask a guy for directions. When I caught up to her, I discovered that she was talking to Scott Jurek. Holy shit! Scott Jurek is a living legend. He's the Michael Jordan of ultramarathoning. He won the Badwater Ultramarathon in 2005 and 2006 and the Hardrock Hundred Mile Endurance Run in 2007. And right behind him was Aron Ralston, the canyoneer who became world famous when he cut off part of his right arm to free himself from a boulder that had trapped him in a canyon in Utah for 127 hours in 2003 (to read about his harrowing adventure, check out his autobiography Between a Rock and a Hard Place). This was like something out of a movie to me. I'd recently listened to the audiobook version of Scott's memoir Eat & Run. I have tremendous respect for both of those men, and the chances of running into the two of them on the AT are infinitesimally small. What a coincidence!

Aron glanced down at my prosthetic leg, and I looked up at his amputated arm. It seemed like we were destined to share stories, but before I could so much as say hi, he took off after Scott, who hadn't seen me because I'd come up behind Sunflower from a side trail. I was a little jealous that she got to talk to Scott.

Days later, I'd learn that Scott had broken a four-year-old record for the fastest ever thru-hike of the AT. He ran nearly 2,200 miles in just forty-six days, eight hours, and seven minutes, which means that he averaged almost fifty miles a day. Think about that. He ran almost two marathons a day for a month and a half straight. The Appalachian Trail Conservancy recommends that hikers take five to seven months to complete the entire trail, but he did it in a quarter of the time. It's hard to fathom the endurance required to run the entire AT in forty-six days, especially for a guy who was forty-one years old. He's a testament to the potential of the human body and the power of the will. And I loved that he wasn't running for a trophy or an endorsement deal from some shoe company. He was running because he loves running. I was lucky to have witnessed a tiny portion of his achievement.

12

LIMPING IN GRANDMA'S FOOTSTEPS

Eight days after starting our hike through the Hundred-Mile Wilderness, I arrived at Monson Slate Hills with Ginger, Tall Legs, and Sunflower. Monson was one of my favorite stops on the AT, in part because I was lavished with attention and with gifts by people I met in town. The owner of the Hostel Joe contacted a local Maine company called Hyperlite Mountain Gear and told them about how badly my back-pack was damaged on my adventure on Katahdin. To my surprise, a representative named Judy sent me a new one (I'd actually met Judy at Trail Days in Damascus, but she wasn't quite ready to sponsor me with a backpack then). Thanks, HMG!

Hyperlite Mountain Gear backpack   Ginger, Me, Sunflower, & Tall Legs

My backpack wasn't the only thing falling apart. My shoes were also in bad shape. They were filled with holes, and both soles had fallen off. I called Adidas and requested a new pair. Once again, they said they didn't mind sponsoring me with some trail runners, and they told me they'd ship the shoes out that same afternoon. I'd have to wait a few days for them to arrive, but I didn't mind sticking around in Monson. It was a lovely little town that treated hikers like kings and queens.

Ginger, Tall Legs, and Sunflower didn't want to wait for my shoes to arrive, so they hiked on without me. I missed my hiking buddies, but there were parties every night in Monson, and I quickly made new friends. It was nice hanging out with other hikers, but after three nights of partying, I was ready to get back on the trail. Relaxing is necessary, and I love a good party, but it's easy to get distracted from your goals if you allow yourself to get swept up in the pursuit of pleasure.

The day after my replacement trail runners arrived, I left Monson with a smile on my face. I loved my fancy new backpack, and my shoes made my good foot very happy. It was also nice to have some quiet time again, and I was ready to do some more night hiking.

But not long after leaving Monson, I discovered that night hiking wasn't as easy in Maine as it had been in Virginia. Maine reminds me of Alaska. There are huge bodies of water everywhere, and the terrain is rugged and unforgiving. The section of the AT from Monson to Caratunk wasn't as difficult as the Hundred-Mile Wilderness, but it was still incredibly challenging. I wasn't hiking so much as scrambling hand over hand along rocky paths, and there were constant elevation changes. Up, down, up, down. I felt like I was either ascending or descending the entire day, and I worried I'd get lost or injured if I tried to hike after sunset. But I did it anyway. I loved the change in scenery. I just had to make sure I moved slowly and took no chances.

The next day, I came across some northbound hikers who told me they'd seen moose along the trail. I was so jealous. Since the day I started hiking the AT, I'd been hoping to see a moose or maybe a majestic elk, but I hadn't seen any big animals yet, unless you count those stuffed and mounted polar bears I saw at a Cabela's store. Seeing large animals in their natural habitat is a special treat for me. On the PCT back in 2006, I saw a giant elk a short distance in front of me, and we maintained eye contact for quite some time, until he slowly walked off into the distance. I was giddy after that experience, and I wanted another one like it. I especially wanted to see a bear, but I hadn't seen one since I saw a grizzly on a highway in Alaska, back when I was riding my motorcycle up to Denali National Park on my way to my EMT training in Haines in 2010.

Grizzly bear, while riding my
bike to Alaska

Polar bear exhibit
at Cabela's store

Landing a job as a ski patroller is challenging because there are so few openings available. I'd applied at several different resorts before I landed a job on one of my favorite mountains in Summit County, Colorado. The only hitch was that I had to get an EMT license. I signed up at a community college in my neighborhood, but I failed miserably, mostly because I couldn't get along with the lecturer. With only a few months left before the winter season started, I searched for a new class. I found a crash course in Alaska. Alaska! I'd always dreamed about riding my motorcycle up there, and the timing was perfect. I contacted the organization that offered the EMT classes, and I made sure the course fit into my timeframe. I was thrilled when I found out that it did. I signed up for the EMT course and for a Wilderness First Responder course as well. I'd have plenty of time to ride up to Alaska, take both courses, and get back home for the ski season.

I left Colorado several weeks before the course started because I wanted to spend some time enjoying the journey to Alaska.

Riding my motorcycle in 2010 to Alaska

I was having a blast driving up there when I got a phone call in British Columbia, Canada. A woman from the organization that provided the courses told me that they'd cancelled the course. My heart sank. My dream job as a ski patroller was disappearing in front of my eyes.

Thinking back on the conversation I'd had weeks ago, I got really upset. "I specifically asked you when I signed up if there was any chance the course would be cancelled, and you promised me that you never ever cancel courses."

"I'm really sorry," she said. "This is totally out of my hands."

I suddenly realized that I didn't know which course she was talking about. "Wait. I signed up for two. Which one got cancelled?"

"The Wilderness First Responder course," she replied.

My heart jumped. Woohoo! I could still get my EMT license!

I told her that I was planning to be in Haines, Alaska, for the duration of the course, including the two weeks that the Wilderness First Responder course was supposed to run, and I explained to her that I was on a budget. I asked her to help me figure out an alternative plan, so I wouldn't have to waste any time or money waiting around for the EMT course to start. She promised she'd get back to me soon.

Me rappelling into a crevasse in Alaska

Several days later, I was hanging out at my uncle's place in Prince Rupert, British Columbia, when I received another call from the organization. The same woman told me that they'd decided to put me in the mountaineering course because of my excellent physical condition, which meant that I'd be sleeping on a glacier for two weeks and learning to rappel into crevasses and climb on ice. And all the gear, tents, and food were included in the original course fee.

What a deal! For no extra cost, I'd get additional training and I'd have a once-in-a-lifetime adventure. That's exactly why you should never give up! Always push on!

"Never give up. Never give in."
~ Bryan Drysdale

That same day I heard about the moose on the AT, I received a text message from a woman who'd reached out to me through Facebook. She said she wanted to meet me, so we arranged to connect at a trailhead that afternoon. She drove for a couple hours from the coast, and she waited for me for several hours. She had snacks and beverages for me and for other thru-hikers. After we chatted on the trailhead for some time, she offered to give me a ride to a tiny town called Rangeley, where I stayed for the night at a hiker hostel. No matter how many trail angels I met, their generosity never ceased to amaze me.

Trail magic on the trailhead in the Rangeley/Stratton area

The next highlight came in a town called Caratunk, where I found a hotel that let thru-hikers use their Jacuzzi. Across from the hotel was a free campsite, and the next morning I had an all-you-can-eat breakfast for only $10. I stuffed myself like it was Thanksgiving dinner. I usually don't eat such a big breakfast, but I needed the calories to make up some of the bodyweight I'd lost over the last several months on the trail. It's always a little difficult to get the body going after a large meal, but it's even more difficult to get a calorie-deprived body moving.

After a relaxing soak at the hot tub the night before and a stuffed belly after breakfast, I crossed the river with a guy whose job it was to ferry people across the Kennebec River. The water of this stretch of the River seems calm and inviting, but the riverbed is lined with slippery, smoothened stones that can send even the surest-footed hiker into the water, which is the last place you want to be with a twenty-something pound backpack strapped over your shoulders. The river is even more dangerous during late summer, when the gates of the Indian Pond dam are opened. The water level increases, and the current can become dangerously strong. A hiker died in the river back in 1986, which is why the ferryman is so important to hikers like me.

A few miles down the trail on the other side of the river, I met a guy named Oli, who rents out log cabins to hikers and tourists. He lives completely off the grid, using a generator to make electricity, and he has no internet access or phone service.

Eating a huge breakfast this morning made me really tired, so I decided to rent a cabin from Oli for the night. It was early afternoon, when I entered the cabin it had a fireplace, so I cooked dinner on the stovetop. I scarfed it down, then immediately fell asleep. I slept for eighteen hours straight. It was much needed rest.

River crossing on the AT with the ferryman

The next morning, Oli made me a huge pancake breakfast and coffee. Back on the trail. I soon came across a volunteer maintenance crew from the Appalachian Trail Conservancy. When you read about the AT, you rarely see anything about the people who make sure that the trail stays safe for hikers, but you really should. They're the unsung heroes of the AT. They take care of the footpaths to reduce sprained ankles. They maintain the lean-to shelters so tired hikers can get the sleep they need to push on. They remove any critters that might pose a threat to hikers. And they do it all for nothing but the love of the trail and the people who hike it. I made sure to thank each one of them individually as I passed them on the path they keep beautiful and safe.

Maintenance crew on the Appalachian Trail

My next week or so was fairly uneventful. I made decent time, even though my leg was really starting to bother me. When I came to the trailhead that led to Rangeley, which is about a hundred trail miles south of Monson, I decided to get a ride into town, so I could sleep under a roof for a night or two. In the parking lot at the trailhead, I saw a woman dropping off a hiker. I asked her if she'd mind driving me into town, and she cheerfully invited me to hop in her car. I loaded my gear into her trunk, and I got in the backseat. I jokingly apologized to her about stinking up her car with my hiker's B.O. She laughed and said that I smelled like a bed of roses compared to her husband after working in the yard. I love all trail angels, but I especially love the ones with a good sense of humor.

The woman took me to a hiker hostel in town, which I later found out was in the exact opposite direction of her house, about ten miles from the trailhead. The place where she dropped me off was called the Farmhouse, and it's owned by a couple named Stacey and Shane. The hostel was incredibly nice. It was spic-and-span clean, and I loved how homey it felt. They let me hang my hammock inside an attached

barn for a fraction of the cost of a room. If there was a downside, it was the sneaky pet guinea pig that knew how to open hikers' backpacks and get into their food supplies, but it was really more of a mascot than a nuisance.

I got settled in, then I headed to the kitchen to make myself a real meal. I was starving for something other than trail mix, oats, pasta, and couscous. I needed something sustaining, something I could sink my teeth into. I opted for a big slab of meat—a juicy T-bone steak—with a baked potato, sour cream, and some veggies on the side. I typically avoid eating meat, but I'd lost much of my body mass on the trail, and I needed something rich in protein and fat. I hate to sound like I'm patting myself on the back, but it tasted incredible. But it wasn't so much my cooking skills that made the meal so delicious as my body's need for food that wasn't beige.

I hung out with some other hikers in the lounge after dinner. The hostel had the largest TV screen I've ever seen. We all watched my favorite movie, *The English Patient*. What a great place. Definitely a great stop on the AT.

I hopped back on the trail after spending a couple days at the Farmhouse. My next resupply stop was in Andover, twenty-something trail miles south of Rangeley. My stump had really started to bother me over the past several months, and my weight loss on the trail wasn't helping matters. I'd lost at least twenty pounds, and some of that weight had come off my stump, which meant that my prosthetic socket didn't fit snugly any more. I'd been using extra socks to fill in the empty space left in the socket, but I'd run out of socks. My prosthetic was loose now, and it was rubbing against the ultra-tender skin, making walking unbearable. I started taking pain killers again, but they weren't strong enough to dull the misery. Toward the end of my walk from Rangeley to Andover, I was limping badly, and the hurt was rubbing away at my will just as the socket was rubbing away at my stump.

Several miles from the trailhead, I ran into a couple hikers who told me that they'd arranged a pick-up from a hostel in Andover, but I wasn't sure I could make it to the trailhead parking lot before the final pick-up time. I was walking at a snail's pace—incidentally, I nicknamed myself the Trail Snail—and there wasn't much light left in the sky. A couple miles before the trailhead, I came across a road. I pulled out my cell phone and called the hostel, hoping they could pick me up from there. Wishful thinking. Before I could even explain my situation to her, she hung up on me. Trail angels are everywhere, but occasionally you do stumble upon a trail devil.

Somehow, I managed to make it those last couple miles to the trailhead. I called the rude woman at the hostel again, and she told me that I'd have to wait a while before she could get me. Her gruff manner irritated me, but I knew better than to snap at her. I needed to be under a roof that night, and she could make my life hell if she wanted to. I swallowed my pride and sat on the side of the road.

I saw several cars while I was waiting. Hoping to catch a lucky break, I held up my thumb when they were close enough to see me. No one stopped, but then I shouldn't have been surprised. I had to take my prosthetic leg off, and that probably wasn't the best look for someone trying to hitch a ride. I had to wait for the woman from the hostel. She showed up several hours after I'd called her. I had to pay an exorbitant price for the ride into town, but it wasn't like I had an option here. I needed to be off the trail, and a ride from this woman was the only way that was going to happen.

I was on crutches again, and it was clear I wasn't going to be able to go any farther on the prosthetic leg I'd been using since Columbia. I needed to get back to Denver, so I could have my prosthetist create a new socket for me. I'd lost about twenty pounds in the past four and a half months, and my stump had atrophied roughly ten percent. So, I called up my friend Maryanne in Miami. She arranged an Airplane buddy pass for me, so I could fly standby to Denver. Flying across the country in the middle of my hike wasn't exactly ideal, but I wasn't going to be able to finish unless I got a socket that reflected the changes in my body mass. For an amputee, walking on an ill-fitting prosthetic is like driving on a flat tire. Not only does it slow you down dramatically, but it also causes structural damage if you travel too far on it. So, I had to take care for it immediately before my body was going to break down.

> "When the world says, "Give up,"
> Hope whispers, "Try it one more time.."
> ~ Unknown

I talked the hostel owner into giving me a—very expensive—ride to the airport in Portland, Maine. I posted a couple pictures on Facebook just before we arrived at passenger drop-off, and I received a text message from a woman who'd befriended me over Facebook. I'd never met her, but she'd been tracking my progress on the AT, and she told me that she worked for a prosthetist in Portland. She said she'd help me get a new socket there, which would save me a trip to and from Denver. If I'd bought my plane ticket, I probably would have refused the offer, but I wouldn't lose any money if I canceled the buddy pass. So, I told the driver we had a change of plans. Besides offering to help me at the prosthetist's office where she worked, she also invited me to stay with one of her friends, a woman named Mary, then she would pick me up the next day. I gave the driver the address to Mary's house, and we headed away from the airport.

When I arrived at Mary's home, she had a hot meal waiting for me at her dinner table. She was excited to hear my story, so between bites, I recounted many of my adventures on the AT. Besides being distracted by the tasty food on my plate, I was preoccupied with Mary's husband, who looked just like Dustin Hoffman. I told him I loved his movies.

He nodded and smiled. "I get that a lot."

"You should probably quit your day job and become his body double," I joked. "And I'll only take a modest finder's fee when you make it big."

I crashed on their couch that night. I think most people hate sleeping on couches, but after sleeping on the ground or in a hammock for months, a couch almost seemed luxurious.

The next day, Mary and her husband took me on a tour of Portland. It was a cute town full of quaint stores, cobblestone streets, and a charming marina. I talked them into stopping at a little beach. I just couldn't resist the call of the waves. I love floating down a peaceful river, but the majesty of the ocean stirs my imagination. That 50-degree water was frigid, but it felt amazing.

Later that afternoon, I finally met Rosie, the woman who worked in a prosthetist's office called Sound Limbs. The prosthetist was on vacation in Canada at the time, but Rosie could get the process started before he returned. I filled out all the required paperwork, then she examined my stump. The skin at the bottom was red and inflamed, and the soft tissue had swollen to twice its normal size. There was no way they could make a cast of the limb in this state, so I'd have to stick around until the swelling subsided. Rosie graciously offered to let me stay at her place until the new socket could be built.

Besides getting the swelling down, I also had to deal with the infection that had again taken root in the bottom of my stump. Rosie recommended that I visit a doctor in Portland to get some antibiotics, but I thought I had a better solution. I called the doctor I'd visited back in Hiawassee, Georgia, and I asked her if I could get a refill on my prescription for antibiotics. She said she was happy to hear that I hadn't given up on my dream of finishing the AT, and she'd gladly fax a prescription to a pharmacy in Portland. I was happy I didn't have to pay the extra money to visit another doctor. When it came to friends and trail angels, I was rich beyond imagination; but when it came to actual money, I was out on a limb.

Over the next week, I spent a lot of time hanging out with Rosie and her three-legged dog (I can't imagine a more suitable dog for a woman working at a prosthetist's office!). She only had to work mornings, so during the afternoon, we saw the sights in Portland and enjoyed some good coffee and some great local microbrewery beer.

The prosthetist returned about a week after I arrived, and he was incredible. He had a wonderful bedside manner, but he also took it upon himself to put me in touch with other companies he thought might be able to sponsor me the cost of the new socket. He gave me the number of a representative at Click Medical. They ended up holding an impromptu fundraiser for me, and they raked in a huge amount of money for the socket. Thanks, Sound Limbs and Click Medical! I might not have been able to finish if not for their support.

Rosie also went to bat for me. She contacted a couple newspapers in Bangor for interviews. She also reached out to a German company called Ottobock in the hope that they could sponsor me with some liners for the socket. That effort dead-ended in the bureaucratic maze that is Germany. She gave up on them and contacted an American company called WillowWood. They didn't hesitate to offer their support, and they sent me all the necessary supplies to get me back on the trail. Thanks, WillowWood!

After two weeks at Rosie's beautiful house, my stump was no longer red and swollen. The rest and the antibiotics had done the trick. I was incredibly thankful for the time I'd spent with Rosie, but I was itching to get back on the trail. When I set out to accomplish something, it's hard for me to relax completely until the task is finished. There's always a voice in my head telling me that I need to get back on the trail, that I need to stop slacking off. So, I told Rosie that it was time for me to push on.

I thanked her for her hospitality and for the support from her company Sound Limbs, then one of her coworkers dropped me off at a hospital near the AT. I arranged a ride from a Couchsurfing host who invited me to stay at her house for a night. While I was waiting for her at the cafe in the hospital, the director of the hospital spotted me. She told me that she recognized me from the front page of her local newspaper. She asked if she could take a couple pictures with me, so she could inspire other amputees at the hospital. I'm never one to pass up a photo op, especially when the photos are for such a good cause.

It was late by the time my Couchsurfing host arrived. Bethany took me to her home, and we cooked a meal together. Then we watched a documentary called *Tracks: A Woman's Solo Trek across 1700 Miles of Australian Outback*. I couldn't have picked a more inspiring movie if I tried. Around that time, I also started listening to an audiobook called *Grandma Gatewood's Walk: The Inspiring Story of the Woman Who Saved the Appalachian Trail*. It was about the first woman to hike the AT by herself. She did it after she turned sixty-five! If those two stories don't motivate you to get out of your comfort zone and try new things, then you might need to check to see if you have a pulse.

Bethany gave me a ride to the trailhead the next morning. As I was getting out of her car in the parking lot, I met a family that was getting ready to hike to Mahoosuc Notch, which is considered the most difficult mile of the AT. I introduced myself to Scott, Courtney, and their three daughters. They told me they were slackpacking a section of the AT (for those who aren't familiar with the term, slackpacking is a hiker expression that means you hand off either all or most of your pack to another person. Without the burden of a pack, you can hike farther and faster). Courtney was driving their car back and forth to their campsite along the trail, so they could have dinner at a restaurant every night. It's not exactly the most strenuous type of hiking, but at least they were on the trail, making memories with their kids.

I wondered if I could somehow yogi them into letting me join them (*yogi*, verb. – to ask strangers you meet on the trail for food, drinks, a car ride, or anything else useful without actually asking). I wanted to participate in their slackpacking adventure, but I didn't want to actually ask them. Like many thru-hikers, I rarely passed up an offer of food, drinks, or a ride, but I also rarely if ever asked other hikers for those things outright (sponsors and friends are definitely exceptions to this rule). As if she was reading my mind, Bethany reached out of her car window and handed over a copy of the local newspaper, which featured me on the front page.

The newspaper article about getting a new prosthetic in Maine

Scott skimmed the article before handing it to Courtney. They looked at each other, then looked at me.

"We'd love for you to join us, but we don't exactly have a lot of spare room in our car," Scott said.

"We'll we make room. She's the Bionic Woman, for God's sake," Courtney replied.

Woohoo! I'd yogi-ed myself into a fun side adventure!

So I said goodbye to Bethany, and I set off with Scott and his girls on the most difficult mile of the entire AT. I left my twenty-some-thing-pound backpack with Courtney, who'd pick us up on the next trailhead. It was nice not having to lug around my pack, especially on this part of the trail. Even without it, the one-mile stretch of the Mahoosuc Notch took us more than three hours. It was constant mountaineering and canyoneering through caves and then up to the next peak.

At Mahoosuc Notch with the family I met at the trailhead

I slackpacked with them for a full five days. Courtney picked us up every night and took us back to the same campground, where I hung my hammock for no charge. And every night we went to a fabulous pub with good food and cold beer. We hiked a decent chunk of the trail together, and I mostly enjoyed hiking without a backpack.

But there was a small part of me that also missed my pack. It felt a little like cheating not to have that extra twenty-something pounds on my back. The masochist in me wanted to suffer, and I felt a little guilty when I wasn't.

But then I was also happy I had the opportunity to test out the temporary socket the prosthetist had built for me until the final product could be delivered on the trail. The test socket was extra strong, which was great, but the socket they were still building for me came with the Boa Dial System, allowing me to tighten and loosen the socket on my stump with ease (Boa also sponsored the cost of the socket the prosthetist in Columbia made for me). I love the dial system, and I appreciate all that Boa, Click Medical and Sound Limbs had done for me.

The family and I eventually went our separate ways, and I was on my own again. My next resupply stop was Gorham, New Hampshire, nearly 300 miles south of my starting point at Mount Katahdin. I had a phone number in my hiking guide for a hostel in Gorham called The Barn. I called and arranged for a free pick-up at the trailhead later that day. I understand that hostels have to make money, and I don't blame them for charging a moderate fee for rides to and from the trailhead, but I really appreciate those hostels that provide free transportation.

As its name suggests, The Barn was an old barn that had been converted into a lodge for weary hikers. It was really cozy. More importantly, the owner of the hostel, Matt, provides slackpacking services. The day after my arrival, he drove me and a couple other hikers to the foot of Wildcat Mountain, which is part of a range called the White Mountains. I left all my gear at the hostel except for some water, a day's worth of food, and my hammock and sleeping bag.

Even without much in my backpack, I had a rough time on Wildcat Mountain. The terrain was steep and rocky, and hiking this section took me more time than I anticipated. I planned for a day, but it ended up taking two. When I made it back to the Gorham trailhead, I contacted Matt and arranged for a pick-up. I was happy to get back to The Barn and rest after two grueling days.

Slackpacking from Wildcat Mountain to Gorham

When I woke up the next morning, my stump was horribly swollen. I was upset that I'd again have to take time off from the trail to recover, but I felt fortunate that my body had the courtesy to wait until I was back in civilization again to revolt. If this had happened to me the day before, when I was on the trail and my cell phone had no reception, I probably would have had to crawl several miles to the trailhead.

I suspected that I was having an allergic reaction to the new liner I received from WillowWood. Besides the grotesque swelling, I had hundreds of little raised dots all over my stump. My leg was an absolute mess.

"Sometimes the smallest step in the right direction ends up being the biggest step of your life. Tip toe if you must, but take the step."
~ Unknown

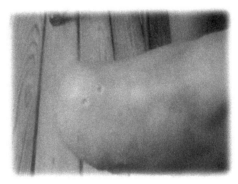

My swollen stump
after slackpacking

What a mess!

I called Rosie back in Portland and told her about my latest setback. She just happened to be on her way to Gorham to watch a cat for a friend who'd left on vacation. What a lucky coincidence! She brought a pair of crutches the next day, and we went to her friend's cabin. Before I went to bed, I got in touch with a Couchsurfing host in the area. I would have loved to have stayed with Rosie back in Portland, but her house was too far away. So, she dropped me off at my Couchsurfing host's house before she left.

For the next several days, I stayed with a host in Berlin, New Hampshire. My stump was in bad shape, so I visited a hospital on the day of my arrival. The doctor performed an ultrasound and diagnosed me with cellulitis, an infection that can cause blood poisoning if not treated properly. He prescribed another course of antibiotics. I wasn't thrilled with the idea of pumping my body full of antibiotics so shortly after my last infection, but the alternative was an infection that could lead to the amputation of more of my leg or to blood poisoning, which can be fatal. No thank you. I wasn't going to risk death. And I certainly didn't want to lose my knee and part of my femur. Being a below-the-knee amputee is plenty challenging enough.

At an ER in Berlin, New Hambshire

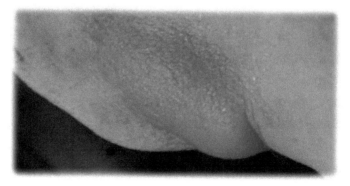

Cellulitis

While I was healing, I sat around doing little but making my host tasty meals and drinking the fancy cocktails my host made for me to help me cope with the pain. Fortunately for me, my body responded well to the medication. After just three days of treatment, the swelling had subsided by about eighty percent. I was getting close to getting back on the trail.

Two other couch surfers were staying at my host's house—one was Austrian, and one was Australian. Half a week into my stay, the Austrian guy decided that he wanted to drive his rental car up to Mount Washington, which is part of the AT. The Australian guy and I decided to go with him just to kill time while my leg healed. The White Mountains are one of the highlights of the AT because the range is mostly above the tree line, which means that you're out of the green tunnel and you can see some amazing vistas.

The Australian and Austrian couch surfers who drove with me
up to the White Mountains

I stayed with my gracious Couchsurfing host until my cellulitis healed. I had to continue my ten-day course of antibiotics, and I still had a wound that I had to treat with antibacterial ointment, but I was now well enough to get back on the trail. It was time to push on.

It had only taken a few hours to drive up the White Mountains, but on foot it took me until dusk before I reached the first hut. The Appalachian Mountain Club owns and maintains huts all along the White Mountains range. At $131 per person per night, the huts aren't exactly the most economical way to hike through the White Mountains, but you do get some perks with the room, including three comfy blankets, a nice dinner, and a big breakfast. I couldn't sleep in a hammock because there are no trees to hang a hammock from above the tree line, but I also couldn't afford to pay $131 to stay in a hut. But if you're a thru-hiker and you're willing to do a little labor, they let you sleep for free on the floor of the dining area. They also feed you what's left over after the paying guests have eaten. And some of the staff put on an improvised theater sketch show after dinner. It was really amusing for us thru-hikers who hadn't watched TV for months.

The first hut on White Mountains   The wound I had to take care of

At another hut called the Lake of the Clouds, I had the option of giving an improvised speech outside the hut to the other hikers and guests in exchange for lodging. I happily stood in front of the small group and shared my story.

Toward the end of my hike through the White Mountains, I stayed at a hut called Lonesome Lake. It was the last one above the tree line, and I was a bit sad that I had to trade the wide-open spaces for the green tunnel again. But the staff at the hut helped me forget my woes for a night by dressing up in costumes and putting on a hilarious skit that had us all doubled over in laughter.

An improvised sketch by the White Mountains crew

I left White Mountains, then spent a few days at a place called the Hikers Welcome Hostel in Glencliff, New Hampshire. The caretaker was friendly, and they had an impressive selection of DVDs for their guests, but they also had a serious fly problem. I swatted flies nonstop for three days.

My stump was swollen again at the end of my trek through the White Mountains, and I needed to rest for several days. I decided to get a ride to Hanover, New Hampshire, from the friend of the caretaker of the Hikers Welcome Hostel. I found a phone number in my hiker's guidebook for families that invited thru-hikers to stay at their homes. I only needed a single phone call to land a friendly family willing to open their home to me. We made plans to meet the next day.

When I showed up, the family wasn't home, but their other guests were there. Two thru-hikers, who'd made their way up from Georgia, showed me to my room and to the bathroom. I cleaned up, then I sat down with them. They said they were exhausted after so many months of hiking, and they were seriously considering quitting the trail. They'd been staying with the host family for more than a week already, and they didn't know if they had the motivation to push on to Maine. They'd been to a local doctor's office for blood work, thinking that they might find out they had some serious ailment that would require them to get on a plane and fly home so as not to endanger their health. But the results came back negative, and they were confronted with the choice of continuing north or heading home.

"Keep improving. Keep pushing. The moment you get comfortsble, you lose."
~ Akin

In my personal experience, I've found that when you take a little break after pushing your body to the max every day for several months, it can be hard to find the motivation to keep going. Your body wants to recuperate, and while it's healing itself, your energy levels are usually low. I've been in that position several times, my mind constantly flirting with the idea of quitting, but I've always managed to find a way to silence those thoughts and get my body moving again. I thought the couple would forever regret the decision to quit when they could practically see the finish line at Mount Katahdin, but then we in the hiking community always say that you have to hike your own hike. No one can make your choice for you, and you have to live with the decision to push on or to fly home. I know what I would have done, but I wasn't sitting in their shoes. It wasn't fair for me to judge them if they decided to quit before finishing the entire trail.

The next day, I went to a movie theater, where I met two AT hikers. Together we watched *A Walk in the Woods*, starring Robert Redford.

It was an adaptation of the book by the same title, which was written by Bill Bryson, who, appropriately enough, lives in Hanover. I know it probably seems silly to some people to watch a movie about hiking the AT while actually hiking the AT, but I was curious to know how Hollywood would depict the challenges of the trail. It made us laugh a couple times, but it wasn't great. It wasn't nearly as impressive as the adaptation of Cheryl Strayed's novel *Wild*, starring Reece Witherspoon. Even that movie wasn't perfect, but they did a much better job in portraying the challenges facing a section hiker on the PCT. (In both movies, the story was about a long section hike, rather than a thru-hike, as they only completed about a third of the trail.)

About to watch *A Walk in the Woods* with other AT hikers in Hanover

I packed up my gear after two days in Hanover and said goodbye to my trail angels. I'd been resting for a total of five days, and the wound on my leg was looking much better. My hosts, Kyle and Sherry, invited me to stay with them again when I came back through Hanover. I suppose they liked my authentic German cooking. I've found that even very generous people are more inclined to invite you back if you tell them to sit down and put their feet up at dinner time and do a little cooking to show your gratitude. I love cooking for people, especially when the hosts invite their friends for a dinner party.

Before I left their home, I opened my magic trail book and found a phone number of a retired guy who offers free rides to hikers. He jumped right in his car and met me over at Kyle and Sherry's house. Then he took me back to the trailhead I'd left a few days earlier.

Over the next couple days, I hiked from Glencliff to a point on the trail near a maple sugar farm. I'd read that the owners of the farm allowed hikers to stay for free, so I decided to hitch a ride to their place. In the parking lot near the trailhead, I dropped my gear and held out my thumb. Not one minute later a car stopped, and a woman hopped out with a huge grin on her face.

"You're the Bionic Woman!" she called out. "I read about you in the paper."

She gave me a warm hug before inviting me to take a seat in her car. While she drove, she peppered me with questions about my adventure, and I did my best to sum it all up before she arrived at the maple sugar farm, only a few miles from the trailhead. And when she pulled over to let me out, she hugged me again and wished me a happy journey. I spent less than ten minutes in her car, but an onlooker who watched her say goodbye to me would have guessed that we were lifelong friends.

The caretaker of the farm gave me a tour of the land and told me I could stay for a night in the little store where the owners sold maple sugar and other souvenirs to tourists. While I was sizing up the shop, my eyes fell upon a picture of Grandma Gatewood, whose story I'd recently listened to as an audiobook on my iPod. I asked one of the owners about the old photo, and he told me the story behind it. When he was just a kid on the farm, his parents answered a knock at their door and discovered an elderly woman wearing a shower curtain over her clothes. They showed her some trail magic, and she was off again the next day. Little did they know that she'd end up becoming a national celebrity and an icon in the hiking community.

Having recently listened to *Grandma Gatewood's Walk*, I knew she's considered the first ultralight backpacker. She used the shower curtain as her only form of shelter, and she'd sewn a bag out of denim to carry what little food and clothing she brought with her. Her bag and her shower curtain weighed a grand total of twelve pounds, about half as heavy as my own pack. I wish I could have gotten away with carrying only twelve pounds on my back, but I likely would have starved if I'd carried so little.

Back when she hiked the trail in 1955, there was no such thing as an AT hiking guide book. There weren't supply pick-up depots where you could mail food and other necessities to yourself. There was no trail book full of phone numbers of people who were known to open their homes to AT hikers. There were no hikers really. Grandma Gatewood was the first woman thru-hiker, and only four men had hiked the entire AT before her. And there actually wasn't really much of an Appalachian Trail to speak of. The AT she hiked was a hodge-podge of roughly made almost-trails that didn't have protection from the federal government. Small hiking clubs maintained short sections of the trail in their region, but they didn't have much money to work with. In other words, as difficult as it is for a person to hike the AT during the second decade of the twenty-first century, it was infinitely more challenging during the middle of the twentieth century. Hikers back in the 1950s couldn't rely on technology or the advice of the hundreds of other hikers who have made the trek before. They had little but sheer determination and trail magic. That was probably the only thing that hadn't changed about the AT since 1955.

When Grandma Gatewood came across a home near the trail, she often knocked on the front door and explained to the home-owners who answered that she was hiking the AT, so posterity would remember her after she died. She'd come across an article in *National Geographic* about the trail, and she decided to become the first woman to thru-hike it. I imagine that the people she talked to probably had a hard time wrapping their minds around the idea of a sixty-seven-year-old grandmother walking from Georgia to Maine simply because she liked a challenge, but that didn't stop them from helping her. In spite of the strangeness of her story, most people invited her into their homes for a warm meal and some rest on an extra bed. She was blazing a new trail as a thru-hiker, but the people she met along the way were also trailblazers of sorts. They were the original trail angels, the inventors of trail magic, and their kindness paved the way for people like the ones who so often bent over backwards to help me achieve my dream. I owe a debt of gratitude to Grandma Gatewood for showing the world that a woman can do anything a man can do and to those pioneering trail angels who established a tradition that has helped so many thousands of hikers like me.

I also have her to thank for the state of the trail. Back then, the AT was a mess, and when she became famous after the media learned of her trek, she often talked of the horrible condition of the trail. After she complained, people and institutions got their acts together and either finished the uncompleted sections of the trail or cleaned up those portions that had been neglected. The trail might not have been the darling of so many organizations if not for Grandma Gatewood.

Carrying on the tradition his parents had helped establish, the owner of the farm made me a tall stack of pancakes the next morning.

They were coated in the maple syrup they harvested a couple hundred feet from where I sat. Talk about a farm-to-table meal! And as if breakfast wasn't already enough, the owner gave me a ride back to the trailhead.

Maple sugar farm in New Hampshire   Grandma Gatewood with the owner

I had another interesting stop on my way back to Hanover. A guy named Bill Ackerly, whom everyone knows as the Ice Cream Man, has a freezer on his back porch full of ice cream, popsicles and sodas, and he allows all thru-hikers to stay on his property and indulge in as many treats as they want. And every once in a blue moon, he digs up his cricket gear and plays a pick-up game with the hikers on his property. He has a reputation for being exceptionally kind to the hikers who find their way to his home, and he lived up to that reputation with me. After he saw the rainbow of mean-looking colors that made my almost-healed stump look so hideous, he offered to take me to the hospital. I turned down his offer because I was full of energy from all the ice cream I ate and the can of Coke I drank, and I wanted to do a night hike.

(After I finished my AT hike, I read in an online hikers' forum that the Ice Cream Man had passed away. I regret not spending an extra day with him. He was such a giving man, and I shouldn't have rushed away from him and his generous heart.)

Hanging out with Bill Ackerly, also known as the Ice Cream Man

I walked into Hanover the next afternoon. On the edge of town, I ran into a group of thru-hikers camping in the woods. They'd just stocked up on beer, and one of the hikers recognized me from a newspaper article and invited me over for a cold one. I wasn't even back in town yet, and already I had some liquid bread in hand!

I drank a couple brews, then some of the hikers got up to leave. They told me they were heading to a belly dancing class that was open to anyone. I can't say that I ever imagined myself belly dancing, but I decided to join them in a sports hall for a free lesson. I felt a little ridiculous at times, but it ended up being a lot of fun.

When the class wrapped up, I contacted Kyle and Sherry, the hosts who'd opened their home to me just a few days earlier. I offered to cook for them again to thank them for their hospitality, but this time they offered to take me to their favorite Asian restaurant. What a treat! At dinner they joked that I should come back and live with them after I finished the AT. *If* I finished, I told them. I'd hiked about 1,250 miles so far, which meant that I had about 950 miles to go. I had the will to keep pushing on, but I didn't know if I had the funds to continue. I was down to my last $100, and I doubted I'd be able to rely on the kindness of strangers for my meals the way Grandma Gatewood had sixty years earlier. Sherry told me not to worry, and she promoted my CrowdRise fundraiser on Facebook.

Trail angels in Hanover

The campaign caught fire. All told, I raised just under $4,500 since I started hiking! Now I'd have no problem finishing the hike. I'm indebted to so many people, and it's important for me to acknowledge all those who helped to ensure that I wouldn't have to quit the trail before finishing. Thanks to Click Medical, Revolimb, Joe Mahon, Jimmy Capra, Paige Boucher, Bulow Orthotic & Prosthetic Solutions, Bobby Latham, Medical Center Orthotics & Prosthetics, Ian Fothergill, the Limb Preservation Foundation, WillowWood, Creative Technology Orthotic and Prosthetic Solutions, Hennessy Hammocks, Hyperlite Mountain Gear, Rosie and Sound Limbs, Adidas, Scoutmaster Troop 63, Form Insoles, Meghan Matthews, Carla "Prada" Akers, Dave and Cara Marcoux, Amanda Clayton, Bob Davis, Danielle Normand, Mike Sauter, Ryan and Kaitlin Servant, Ak Gina, Jeffrey Jones, Ted Light, Duncan Fordyce, Scout Troop 344, Ryan Lamonde, Betty Buhr, Dr. Michael Mahon, Joe Mahon, Pan Wilson, Alex Shoer, Simone Havel, Inside Out PR, Francois Lefebvre, Warren Weiss, Tom Jones, Paul Stevens, Dean Brooks, Courtney Allen, and all the other anonymous supporters and total strangers who helped me get to the finish line. A million thanks!

13

RANDOM ACTS
OF KINDNESS

When I crossed the state line and stepped into Vermont, I had officially visited every state in the US. I'd spent the better part of a decade exploring as much territory as possible, and now I could say that I was part of a smallish group of people who'd stepped on the soil of all fifty states.

To be able to accomplish this milestone, I hiked the PCT and AT, bicycled across the country three times, and rode a motorbike across the country twice, as well from Colorado to Alaska and back. I also rode my bicycle from Alaska to Mexico City over a two-year period and cycled around Puerto Rico and Hawaii. That feels like kind of a cool milestone for someone who has only been in the US since 2002, with a couple of years in-between back in Germany.

I was immediately impressed by the beauty of the landscape and the people of Vermont. It was close to sunset when I first stepped foot in the state. A woman who was on a day hike caught up to me, and we talked for quite a while. When we got to the trailhead where Sally had parked her car, she invited me to stay overnight at her place. As usual, I jumped at the offer.

The next morning, she invited me to stay for an extra day, and I again accepted her generous offer. Because I now had a little extra time to spare, I decided to contact a guy who'd reached out to me over Facebook and asked me to get in touch with him when I made it to Vermont. He was a snowboarding coach for disabled people in the state. His house was only a few miles from Sally's place, and he picked me up and took me out to his wife's pub, for a nice evening. After a few hours of eating, talking, and drinking beers, he took me back to my host's house.

Sally gave me a ride back to the trailhead early the next morning. There was a steep uphill climb just past the trailhead, and I burned a bunch of calories pushing my way up to the top. At the peak of the hill, I met a young girl who was hiking with a husky. We talked for a few minutes, then we went our separate ways.

About forty-five minutes later, I heard her husky come trotting up behind me. He stopped and sat on the trail, staring at me from a distance. I figured that the girl must be close behind him, so I turned and continued walking south. A few minutes later, I heard something in the distance, and I looked back and saw the same dog. He seemed to be following me like a shameless stalker. I yelled at him to leave and waved my arms at him in the hope that he'd run back to his owner, but he just sat on the trail and peered at me. I have a soft spot in my heart for dogs, so I walked back to him. I assumed that he must have gotten away from the young girl who'd been with him, and I guessed that he'd latched on to me because he remembered seeing me back on the top of the mountain, where I'd met him with his owner. I hadn't owned a dog in years, but if I did own one, I'd hope that someone would track me down if I got separated from the furry guy.

The husky on the AT

I approached the dog cautiously, in case he wasn't as friendly as he appeared. A few feet away from where he sat, I knelt down and held my hand out for him to smell. He got up, walked over to me, and licked my fingers. He was a big teddy bear, a gentle giant. I grabbed his collar and found his owner's phone number. I called and got voicemail. A few minutes after I left a message, I received a text from the girl asking me to hold on to her dog until she could hike to me (What is it with Millennials and their love of text messages?!). The trailhead was about three miles back from where I stood, and I didn't love the idea of backtracking, but I thought she'd appreciate it if I met her halfway. So, I reached into my backpack and dug out a rope for my hammock. I looped it through a metal ring on the dog's collar to use as a leash, and together we headed back up the mountain I'd just descended.

While I walked, I remembered Anka, a German Shepherd my grandfather had owned on his farm when I was a child. I loved that dog, almost as much as that dog seemed to love me. My grandfather, on the other hand, had a strained relationship with Anka. I grew up on his farm, next to the house where my parents ran a family restaurant. Every day after school, I played with Anka. She obeyed my every command, but she ignored everything my grandfather said. One day I showed up to play with Anka after school, and both she and my grandfather were gone. When I asked my parents where they were, my mother told me that my grandfather had sold Anka to a couple who lived more than thirty miles away. I was devastated, and I went to my room and cried like a baby. I couldn't believe that my grandfather had sold the dog my brother and I loved so much, and I couldn't understand why he hadn't given me a chance to say goodbye to her, or why he didn't just let my brother and me keep her.

I had a good cry before my parents came up to my room and told me they knew the address of the people who'd bought Anka. I begged them to take me, so I could get her back. It took us close to an hour to drive all the way out to Anka's new home. When we got there, I jumped out of the car, expecting her to come running up to me, but Anka was nowhere in sight. We talked to the new owners, and they told us that she'd run away just hours after my grandfather dropped her off. A couple days later, she found her way back to my grandfather's farm, more than thirty miles away. Rather than returning her to the couple who'd bought her, my grandfather gave them their money back and gave Anka to my brother and me, and we took care of her for the rest of her life.

I had a special bond with that dog, one that lasted right up until the day she died. When she was about thirteen years old, she developed a huge cancerous ulcer on her belly, but she was much too old for surgery. For the last couple weeks of her life, she hid in my grandfather's barn, and every day after school I checked on her. On the day she died, I found her panting and whining. I petted her head and told her how much I loved her. Just minutes after my arrival, she closed her eyes and stopped breathing. It seemed like she'd been waiting for me to show up, so we could see each other one more time before she passed. That was the first time I ever really encountered death, and the vivid image of that limp dog lying in my arms has stayed with me to this day.

The Millennial with the husky she lost on the trail

Not long after I reached the summit with the husky in tow, I heard approaching footsteps. I looked up and saw the woman walking with a man, who turned out to be her father. They were both ecstatic that I had the dog with me, and they showered him with hugs before inviting me to dinner in their home to show their appreciation for finding their dog. I gratefully accepted the invitation.

While we were walking to the trailhead parking lot, I asked the guy, who's name was John, how far the Manchester airport was from where we were.

"Manchester doesn't have an airport," he said.

"But I have a ticket from Manchester," I replied.

"Do you mean Manchester, New Hampshire?"

Shitty shit! How had I not realized that Vermont and New Hampshire both have a city named Manchester? And whose idea was it to use the name for two cities that are only 120 miles apart (by car)? I'm sure I'm not the only person who has made that mistake.

I had to fly back to Denver for a visit to my prosthetist's office to have my new socket fitted properly and for a court hearing I hadn't been able to make while I was in rehab back in Germany after my accident. I'd booked a standby ticket through Maryanne (my friend in Miami) from Manchester to Denver, but she must have misunderstood me when I told her I was in Vermont, and I had no idea there were two Manchester's so close to each other.

"I guess I have to get a rental car to New Hampshire," I told John.

"No need. I'll give you a ride," he replied.

My eyes became saucers. "Really?"

He grinned. "It's the least I can do to thank you for finding our pup. And I have to drive up north for work anyway. I can swing by the airport and drop you off. If you can wait for two days."

I arranged for a ride two days south, on the trail from Sally, the day hiker I'd met near the Vermont border. John offered to pick me up from Sally's house. It boggles my mind sometimes when I think about how generous people are to complete strangers out on the trail. I wish I could bottle that goodness and save it for difficult days.

As promised, John picked me up from Sally's house two days later. We had a lot of time to talk while we drove north, and John told me all about his job as a structural engineer scuba diver. It's a fascinating profession that I didn't even know existed. Apparently, he gets contracts all up and down the East Coast to use his welding equipment to perform underwater repairs on bridges and other structures. It sounded like an amazing job, and I have to admit that I was a little jealous of his work. He was keeping people safe while also working in nature every day—what a gig!

We arrived at the airport with plenty of time to spare, so after I checked in, I pulled out my phone and logged on to Facebook. I posted a request for a pick-up at the Denver airport, and within minutes I had a reply from a couple I'd met at the Woods Hole Hostel in Pearisburg, Virginia. It turned out that they lived close to the Denver airport and they'd gladly pick me up. They also offered to let me crash at their place for a few days while I got things sorted out with my prosthetic and my court hearing.

My visit to Denver was a whirlwind. I hung out a little with the couple who picked me up and opened their home to me, I caught up with a few friends, and Zach Harvey and his team adjusted my prosthetic, so it wouldn't—fingers crossed!—cause me any more trouble for the rest of my trip. It was nice being back in Denver, but I also couldn't wait to leave. I didn't like being so far from the AT. This taste of home felt premature. This was where I was going to come back after I was done hiking, and it didn't feel right to be spending time relaxing there before my walk to recovery was done.

On my way back to the East Coast, one of my very good friends, Matt, who was with me the day I shattered my leg in that canyoneering accident, told me via Facebook that he was visiting his brother in Maine. He said he'd give me a ride back to the trail, but I'd have to do a little traveling first to get to him. After landing in Boston, I took a bus to Salem, where he and his brother picked me up. We had a lovely dinner with his whole family, and we talked a lot about that day that so drastically altered the course of my life. The next morning, Matt and I drove a rental car back to the trailhead in Manchester (Vermont, that is), and together we hiked for the better part of the day.

Hanging out with Matt, the good friend who drove me back
to the AT and hiked with me for a day

I was very happy with how my newly adjusted prosthetic felt. It was snug and comfortable, and the bottom of my stump didn't rub on the socket at all. I had about 860 miles to hike back to where I'd left the trail in Glasgow, Virginia, and I felt great. The rest had done wonders for my mind and my body, and I was full of energy when Matt and I parted ways.

A couple days after getting back on the trail, I received a message through Facebook from High Noon, the guy I'd gone aqua blazing with in Virginia. He'd seen one of my Facebook posts where I'd complained about how cold I was in my hammock at night. Summer had faded, and I was now in the thick of autumn, and with the changing of the leaves came a biting cold that chilled my bones in the dead of night. High Noon sent me a link to a company that makes down under quilts for hammocks. The quilts looked perfect for my needs, but there was no way I could afford to pay more than $200 to buy one. On a whim, I sent them an email explaining my journey on the AT, and without asking a single question, they told me they'd ship a quilt out to me free of charge. Thanks, Jacks 'R' Better! That quilt kept me nice and toasty through many cold nights on the trail.

This quilt from Jacks 'R' Better kept me warm on cold nights

The next week was fairly uneventful, which was a good thing given how much time and effort I'd put into getting that new socket. Difficult and dramatic hiking makes for a good story after you've finished the AT, but I'd take smooth and boring hiking any day of the week. You'd probably like to hear about how I woke up in the middle of the night to discover a bear eating my food and beat it over the head with my prosthetic leg until it ran away with its tail between its legs. But that didn't happen. I woke up feeling rested, I put a long day of hiking in, then I ate and went to sleep. While hiking the AT is a bucket-list adventure for many people, the truth is that most days are repetitive. Yes, you're surrounded by nature at its most splendid, but when you hike through all that beauty day after day after day, much of it starts to look the same. I'm not complaining, though. Not too long ago, I thought the infection in my leg might keep me from finishing my hike. I was happy to have a string of unexciting, pain-free days.

I hiked with two chicks their name was Tina and Zoey on and off for the following few days. We'd met for the first time in the White Mountains, and after they left me behind, I thought I'd never see them again. But they liked to take really long breaks on the trail, and I caught up with them somewhere in Massachusetts. I always thought that I was the slowest of the trail snails, but it turned out that they weren't making much better time than I was. I guessed that there was a good chance I'd go down in history as the person with the slowest AT hiking time for 2015, but I had serious competition with Tina and Zoey.

We hiked together for the rest of that day, then we left the trail for the night to find a pub to celebrate Zoey's twenty-seventh birthday. We had several drinks in a tiny town, but we couldn't stay out too late because we still had to find a place to camp. It was dark and chilly, and we weren't in the mood to hike too far, so we found a cow pasture next to a busy road and set up camp there. It wasn't the best sleeping spot, but the drinks helped me fall asleep quickly.

The next day, I received a text message from a woman named Amanda, who was following my progress on Facebook. She invited me to stay at her house for a night. I gladly accepted her invitation. It was raining steadily that day, and I was thrilled with the prospect of spending a dry night in a warm house. I texted her back and asked if Tina and Zoey could crash with me. She said she was delighted to have us, and we made arrangements to meet at a trailhead later that day.

When we got to Amanda's house, I discovered that Tina, Zoey, and I weren't the only guests invited to stay for the night. Amanda had been out hiking the day before, and she came across a coyote that was just starting to chow down on a live chicken. Amanda chased away the animal, saving the lucky bird's life. The chickens back looked like it had been plucked, and there were some nasty teeth marks in the bird's flesh, but she thought it would live. So, she turned her home into a sanctuary for partially eaten fowl. She intended to let the bird live out its days in her backyard. Except when it was raining, as it was that day. Amanda thought the chicken would be more comfortable spending the night in her bathroom, so I had to shower with the bird in there. I've done a lot of things in my life, but that was the first time I've ever showered in front of a chicken. But then I guess that was probably the first time the chicken had ever watched a German chick take a shower.

I freshened up and wished the chicken a good night, then I made some hot wine called Gluehwein, a German favorite on rainy days. It's always nice to have a warm drink in your hands when it's cold outside, and it's especially nice when that warm drink has a little booze in it. We all had a glass before heading out for dinner at a bar and grill that had a mechanical bull in the middle of the restaurant. Riding that bull was quite a change of pace for me. It certainly wasn't something I envisioned doing while hiking the AT.

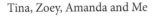

Tina, Zoey, Amanda and Me | Chicken recuperating after being rescued from a hungry coyote

I got back on the trail the next morning. Tina and Zoey wanted to go back into town to have coffee, so I left them behind and pushed on. I figured I'd see them again. And if not, we could keep in touch on Facebook to figure out who set the record for the slowest thru-hike that year. (I'm happy to say that they took the title of Trail Snail 2015, finishing about two months after I did. Congrats, Tina and Zoey!)

While I was hiking through a town called Great Barrington, a couple approached me and asked if I was a thru-hiker. I told them I was, and they invited me to crash at their place that night. During our conversation on the car ride to their home, it became clear that they were very familiar with the AT. I asked them if they'd spent much time on the trail. They told me that they'd learned everything they knew from the thru-hikers they regularly kidnapped. They knew how much we hikers appreciate a warm shower and a soft bed after a long day of hiking, and they often opened their home to people like me. The icing on the cake was that they took me out to dinner at a microbrewery. I love that some people are always looking for a way to express their generosity on the trail!

I crossed the state line and stepped into Connecticut two days later. On that first day in Connecticut, I received a call from a ski instructor friend who lives in Summit County, Colorado, near Keystone, where we worked as ski instructors back in 2009. He told me he'd gone to a private Massachusetts boarding school called Berkshire School, and he'd contacted them about my hike. They thought my story could help inspire their students to push on after experiencing setbacks, so they invited me to give a speech in front of the high school students. A few hours after I agreed to give a talk, a woman from the school drove more than a hundred miles to kidnap me and drive me to Sheffield, Massachusetts.

I'm not sure what exactly I was expecting when I walked onto the school grounds, but I certainly wasn't anticipating such a remarkable campus. It looked like a mini university, with its stately buildings and grassy open spaces. I was surprised to learn that the school's athletic center included a hockey rink, but I was downright shocked to discover that yearly tuition is $59,000. $59,000! For a person who grew up in a country where you can get an excellent college education at a public university for just a few hundred dollars a semester, it's hard for me to imagine spending nearly a quarter of a million dollars to put a child through high school.

When my friend asked me to speak at the school, I assumed I'd be talking in a classroom setting, but I soon discovered that they had their own theater, and they led me to a stage in front of five hundred-something people, all gathered to listen to me a student and a teacher.

The student was a girl named Insha Afsar, a sophomore who'd lost her left leg when she was five during an earthquake in Pakistan. She was a member of the school's championship downhill ski team, and she said she dreams of competing in the Paralympics one day. The teacher was a woman named Sydney Satchell, who lost part of her left leg in a car accident the year before. Both the student and the teacher told inspirational stories, and I count myself lucky that I got to share a stage with them.

My speech at Berkshire School in Massachusetts

The students and the faculty in attendance gave us a standing ovation after we finished. Listening to their applause, I wondered if I could maybe make a living out of motivational speaking after I finished hiking the trail. People seemed to appreciate my story about ignoring bad advice from doctors, friends, and family and pushing on after adversity strikes. It is important to listen to yourself, to figure out what you want to do. It's the only way to stay motivated and not end up in depression or feel sorry for yourself.

I received my first paycheck as a motivational speaker that day, and I spent a restful night in a comfortable hotel. The next morning, the woman who kidnapped me from the trail brought me back to the same trailhead in Connecticut, and I was once again on my way south.

The Connecticut stretch of the AT is only about fifty miles, and I was through the state in half a week. The day I arrived in New York, I hopped on a train close to the trail and I headed to Manhattan. My hiker friends Celtic and Tiny Feet—I met them back in the Hundred-Mile Wilderness in Maine—had invited me to crash at their place when I was in the area, and I decided to take them up on their offer. It had been more than a decade since I'd visited the Big Apple, and I missed the city's energy. I wanted to take in the sites for a couple days and share some time with a couple I'd really enjoyed talking with on the trail.

The station where I boarded a train to NYC

I arrived in New York City during one of the best times of the year: Halloween. Not only did I get to watch adults run around the city dressed like cartoon and comic book characters, but I got to stand on the sidelines of the New York City Marathon, cheering on the runners as they took part in one of the world's biggest marathon events. Back in Germany at the turn of the millennium, a good friend and I kicked around the idea of flying to New York to run the marathon, but to get a running number, you had to pay a ridiculous price to book an all-inclusive package. Or you have a fast-qualifying time. I'd recently finished the Berlin Marathon in less than four hours, but even that didn't make the cut.

So instead I booked myself a flight to Vancouver, Canada, to bicycle to Alaska. During those years from 2002 to 2004, I bicycled over 15,000 miles exploring North America.

> "Life is like riding a Bicycle. To keep your balance, you must keep moving."
> ~ Albert Einstein

Watching the New York City Marathon

I love both the spectacle of Halloween and the grandeur of the NYC Marathon, but my favorite part of my stay was watching *Misery* by Stephen King on Broadway. The show starred Bruce Willis as Paul

Sheldon, and he lost himself so convincingly in the character that I had a hard time recognizing him. Or maybe it was just that I was used to seeing him with a totally bald head rather than with shaggy sides and nape. But all my doubts were quickly dispelled when I saw his security crew and his stretch limo outside after the show.

I left New York City after a few days of R&R, and I took the train back to the trail. A couple days later, I arrived at Bear Mountain State Park, which is just west of the Hudson River. The Bear Mountain Lodge sits close to scenic hiking trails and is a mile from the Hudson River. A woman named Joan had befriended me on Facebook, and she invited me to stay at the lodge, where she worked as a manager. I loved the rustic look of the place, and it had some spectacular views of the Hudson, especially from the lounge. I had a fabulous dinner there, and Joan put me in a homey room that night. Thanks, Joan!

While at the lodge, I met a fascinating woman named Alba (I loved the blue hair, Alba!). She lives in New York City, and she told me that she was directing a short stop-motion animated film about siblings who get separated, only to be reunited years later. She said it was a story about hope and faith, and it was clear that she was excited about the project. But she also said that it was difficult to break into the animated film industry, and it seemed like she wasn't sure she'd be able make a place for herself in the business. She told me that she thought my hike was inspirational, and she needed some inspiration, so she could push on in her work. I looked her up months later to find out how she was doing, and I discovered that she'd won several awards for her work on her third short film. Congrats, Alba!

The day after I left the lodge, I met with another woman who'd befriended me through Facebook. Her name is Brooke, and she's a prosthetist who lost her leg when she was a child. She'd been following my story, and she reached out to me because we were sisters in amputation, and she'd also been dreaming about hiking the AT on her prosthetic. Of all the people who told me that they admired me for what I was doing, Brooke's praise probably had the most meaning for me. She knew exactly what sorts of challenges I faced daily. She understood me better than anyone else I'd met.

The timing of Brooke's appearance in my life couldn't have been better. Just the day before she picked me up from a trailhead, I was doing a night hike, and some of the screws on my prosthetic loosened while I was descending a steep hill. My foot detached from my socket mid stride, and I face-planted on the ground. I'm still not sure how I avoided getting hurt. As I brushed myself off and examined my body for breaks, I looked to my right and saw a big boulder next to me. If I'd hit my head on that rock, I probably would have been knocked unconscious. This happened about 2 a.m., so I likely wouldn't have been found until the next morning. I double- and triple-checked myself for injuries because adrenalin was coursing through my body, and pain is easy to overlook in such an excited state. But I seemed to be fine. I'd been extremely lucky.

When I knew my body wasn't broken, I turned my attention to my prosthetic. There was no way I could find the screws in the middle of the night, but I couldn't walk without a foot. I remembered the duct tape I'd wrapped around my hiking poles, and I used it to secure the foot to the socket. The foot wasn't exactly securely attached, but it worked in a pinch. Somehow, I managed to get down the rest of that hill and find a place to hang my hammock. I was scheduled to meet Brooke at a nearby trailhead the next morning, and it seems crazy to me that I'd meet a prosthetist just hours after my prosthetic leg fell to pieces. What are the odds of that happening? I'd guess that they're miniscule.

Brooke took me to her office, so we could replace the missing screws. She also gave me several replacements, just in case. As I've said before, it's not easy finding metric screws in the US, so it was nice to have spares.

We took some pictures showing off our prosthetics, then we left her office and went straight to the MetLife Stadium in East Rutherford, New Jersey. She had an extra ticket for a Jets game, and it had my name all over it. I'm not a huge football fan, at least not the American version of "football," but I had a blast with Brooke and her family, especially while we tailgated before the game.

We ate a huge, calorie-laden meal after the game, then I got a good night of sleep. Brooke took me back to the trailhead the next morning. As always, I was sad to part ways with my new friend, but I was looking forward to get back on the trail because I could smell the finish line. I had just under 600 miles left, and I wanted to finish before Christmas. I had to average more than ten miles a day to make it, but that wasn't an impossible goal. And what better way to celebrate the biggest holiday of the year than to cross that imaginary finish line? It would be the best possible gift I could give to myself.

I headed south again, and I soon met a guy named Randy, who was also working on a flip-flop thru-hike. We walked and chatted for most of that day, and sometime near dusk, we came across a father and his ten-year-old son. The boy had just shot a deer for the first time, and his father was teaching him how to gut the animal. Randy and I watched as the man instructed his son about how to slit open the deer's belly and about how to cut out the organs properly. Randy was in awe of the whole gory scene. He was a city boy who'd never seen an animal butchered. I'd gutted more animals than I could recall in my lifetime, starting as a child, so it was old hat to me. I was more interested in Randy's reaction to the butchering. I watched him in fascination as he watched the deer being gutted.

I met Randy at the tail end of his hike. He only had another hundred-something miles to go, but he decided to quit before he finished. I thought he was crazy to walk away when he was so close to his finish line, but I didn't say anything to him. He reminded me of another

Dad and his son hunted a deer

hiker I'd encountered on the PCT back in 2006. The guy was only a few hundred miles from the end of the trail near Manning Provincial Park in British Columbia, Canada, but he woke up one rainy morning and decided to throw in the towel. I tried to talk him out of quitting, but he was done. I remember feeling so sad for him as he walked away from the trail to hitch a ride on the nearest highway. But as I've said before, you have to hike your own hike. Only you have to live with your decision to quit. Everyone who attempts a thru-hike has these thoughts, and the best advice I can give to hikers is that you shouldn't quit on a miserable day. If you're going to walk away from the trail, don't do it when it's raining or when the wind is blowing hard. If you have to quit, do it on a sunny day, if you still want to quit when it is a pleasant day.

"You never fail until you stop trying."
~ Albert Einstein

Like most thru-hikers, I flirted with the idea of quitting the trail several million times, but a lifetime of athletic training prevented that from happening. I know what regret feels like, and I hate that feeling. I often thought about abandoning the trail, so I could sleep in a comfortable bed in a cozy room, but I knew that regret would start nagging at me before I even got out of bed on that first morning away from the trail. And that regret would never leave me alone for the rest of my life. If I walked away from the trail, I'd probably feel sick every time I heard the words "the Appalachian Trail." To know that I'd almost made it to the end, but I'd quit not because I was injured so badly that I couldn't walk but because my mind was weak—I just couldn't handle that disappointment.

Randy got me thinking about how I'd feel when I finished the AT. Completing the PCT back in 2006 was quite the celebration. About fifty miles before Manning Park, some previous thru-hikers had left a note of encouragement and some bottles of champagne at a trailhead so thru-hikers—but not yellow blazers, the note read—could party at the finish line. It was a blast shaking up that bottle and pouring it over my head that last day on the PCT.

But that was a completely different experience. Hiking the AT was far more taxing for me, and I had some significant setbacks due to my accident. I wasn't sure how I was going to feel at the end, but I expected that I'd be even more euphoric than I'd been after finishing the PCT.

On our fourth day of hiking together, Randy and I crossed into Pennsylvania, a state known for its rocks. We split a hotel room for the night. Randy's dad picked him up the next morning, and I was on my own again.

I put my head down and plowed through the following days. I was sad to see Randy go, but I've never had a problem traveling on my own. In my many travels, I've spent weeks and sometimes even months on my own, and I think it's an important life lesson to figure yourself out, by yourself, with no one to distract you. I truly believe that no one can enjoy your company if you don't enjoy your own company.

It was the middle of autumn at this point. While the sun was up, the hiking was good, and I made respectable time. But when the sun set, and the warmth drained from the day, I froze my butt off. The under quilt that Jacks 'R' Better mailed to me was a tremendous help in keeping the worst of the cold out of my bones, but it still wasn't fun sleeping in temperatures that plunged into the teens in the wee hours of the night. And it wasn't like I was wrapped in that cozy quilt from the second the sun set until the moment the sun rose in the morning. I think it's enough to say that it's not fun squatting behind a bush in freezing temperatures in the middle of the night.

My hammock, on the trail in freezing temperatures

Except for my battle with the cold, the next week was smooth sailing. I hiked ten to fifteen miles a day, and my stump was in good shape. It would be misleading to say that my days were totally pain free, but the pain was manageable. I was feeling confident that I'd be able to finish before Christmas.

About a week after I left Wind Gap, I passed into Berks and Schuylkill County in Pennsylvania. A woman named Dina kidnapped me from the trail and took me to her place for a hot meal and a warm bed. For the next few days, she treated me to some much-appreciated slackpacking. She would take me to the trail in the morning and pick me up south of my starting point shortly before dusk (she liked to hike toward me on the trail and hike back to her car, so she could get some exercise in every day). Then she let me crash at her place at night. She absolutely spoiled me for a couple days.

The best part of being kidnapped from the trail in the middle of autumn, aside from the companionship, was the warm bed I got to sleep in at the end of the day. Nights were damn cold before I spent those days sleeping in Dina's spare bedroom, but they felt even more brutal when I started sleeping on the trail again. The best decision I made on the AT was to do a flip-flip thru-hike. I can only imagine how miserable my nights would have been toward the end of my hike if I'd been traveling north at this time of year rather than south.

But lucky for me, I didn't have to spend many nights outside before another trail angel reached out to me. The story of my hike was starting to spread around the internet about this time. People were posting my phone number on various social media geared to hikers and to trail angels who lived near the AT. I started getting tons of texts and Facebook messages from people offering to kidnap me for a night, so I wouldn't have to sleep under the stars. They also wanted to hike with me for part of the day, which I loved. Sharing stories with a fellow hiker is a great way to make the miles fly by. A couple nights after staying with Dina, I crashed at the home of a woman named Kim, who spent the better part of a day on the trail with me.

I appreciated all the hot meals, the engaging conversation, and the warm beds on those bitterly cold nights, but all the attention was also starting to intimidate me a bit. When I met people, they talked about what an honor it was to meet me in person. I knew that what I was trying to do was something no other woman had done before, but I suppose I didn't think that so many people would be interested in my hike. At one point, the Facebook app on my phone showed that nearly 56,000 people were talking about me on Facebook. And newspaper articles were popping up left and right in the cities and towns near the trail. A friend back in Denver even told me that he had seen me on TV in a replay of the interview I'd given in Damascus.

I figured that people were too busy with their lives to focus on some German-American chick hiking the AT, but I was mistaken. People were really excited that I was getting close to the end of my journey, and their excitement was contagious. I was trying not to get too excited, though. I still had a lot of miles ahead of me, and there was plenty that could go wrong. I didn't want to start counting my chicks before they hatched.

A park ranger who followed my progress on Facebook found me on the trail. He contacted another AT ranger named Liz, and she invited me to the Appalachian Trail Museum in Garners, Pennsylvania. The museum was closed for the remainder of the year, but she offered to give me a private tour of the place and to let me stay at her house for the night. As usual, I cooked dinner to show my appreciation for her generosity.

The park ranger who found me on the AT by following my progress on Facebook

Her adopted son was visiting from Washington, DC, that night, and he told me that he worked at the White House. His job was to read all the letters from people who wanted to meet President Obama. His tales made for an amusing evening.

The AT Museum was way more remarkable than I expected it to be. It's inside a 200-year-old grist mill, and it's the only museum in the US dedicated exclusively to hiking. There was a bunch of information about some of the earliest thru-hikers, including Earl Shaffer and Grandma Gatewood. Admission is free, so I encourage everyone to drop by when in the area.

On the Appalachian Trail near the AT Museum

Toward the end of the month, a woman named Cindy invited me to Thanksgiving dinner. We'd slackpacked together for several days, and she wanted me to celebrate the holiday with her family at a wonderful restaurant. The day after Thanksgiving, she held me hostage and took me to a dinner party with a scout troop. The troop was planning a section hike of the AT the following year, and the scouts asked me all kinds of questions about my experiences on the trail. I think most of them were shocked by how long a thru-hike actually takes, even for someone who doesn't face all the challenges I faced. A couple weeks after that dinner, the troop and I ended up in their local newspaper.

The scout troop I dined with the day after Thanksgiving

The newspaper article

A UPS truck delivered my new foot to Cindy's house the next morning. I felt like a kid opening a Christmas gift as I took it out of the box. It was a Vari-Flex XC Rotate, a fancy new model designed by a company called Oessur for people like me who can't stop moving. I immediately tried it on and discovered that it was a few inches too long. Cindy's dad just happened to be a mechanic, and he offered to make the necessary adjustments to my prosthetic leg, so it fit properly. He had it fixed in no time.

My new foot was finally delivered by UPS

Prosthetic adjustments by Cindy's dad

The wear and tear of the trail had been too much for my old prosthetic foot. Like a hiker whose body betrays him, the foot just didn't have what it takes to finish the AT. But now I had a new foot, and able to finish what I started.

14

ON MY LAST LEG

I had about 350 miles left when I got back on the trail after Thanksgiving, and I was hoping to be done in just under a month. That seemed like an achievable goal. At the rate I was moving, I figured I'd actually have a chance to walk into Glasgow a couple days before Christmas. That prospect helped me get going on those cold mornings when my blood moved like molasses.

The day after getting my new leg, Cindy and I visited a famous hiker hostel called the Doyle in a little town named Duncannon. Cindy and I had lunch, then we jumped on the trail. I was trying to get fourteen miles in that day, including half a dozen miles during a nighttime hike. Cindy hiked with me for the rest of that day and for several more days after that.

After Cindy and I parted ways, another trail angel named Jen opened her home to me. I stayed with her for the next three nights. Her generosity allowed me to slackpack my way through the rest of Pennsylvania and through most of Maryland. The Maryland leg of the AT is really short, just forty-one miles. Jen picked me up from a designated trailhead toward the end of each of those three days, fed me a home-cooked meal, then pointed me toward the bedroom. I loved that these trail angels kept me indoors during those frigid nights. One of the biggest downsides of sleeping outside during the winter is that you have to eat a lot more because of all the shivering you do at night (the general rule of thumb is that if you wake up shivering, you should eat a candy bar). When you shiver, your body is using energy to create warmth, and you have to feed that furnace with extra fuel. If you don't, then you exhaust yourself, which makes for miserable hiking. But because my trail angels were making sure I was sleeping inside as much as possible during this final leg of my hike, I didn't have to load up on calories to keep me going during the day. It saved me money because I didn't have to buy a bunch of extra food, and I also didn't have to carry the extra weight in my pack. That was just one of many ways they made my life less unpleasant on those cold December days and nights.

I spent three nights at Jen's house before she dropped me off at Gathland State Park. That day, I hiked to Harpers Ferry in West Virginia, the place I'd left the trail to drive up to Mount Katahdin in Maine. Because I'd aqua blazed from Glasgow to Harpers Ferry, I didn't consider my hike done until I reached the place where High Noon picked me up in Glasgow. Still, arriving at Harpers Ferry was awesome because I could take another picture at the sign that marks the midway point of the trail. Not to mention that their office had free Wi-Fi and computers, for thru-hikers. And there was a blackboard where trail angels could post notes to hikers who needed a place to crash. While I was sitting in the lounge, a trail angel walked in and invited me to stay overnight in her spare guest room.

My second visit to the AT Conservancy at the midway point of the AT

The day after my visit to Harpers Ferry was my forty-first birthday. I loved the idea of spending my birthday in the town considered the psychological midpoint of the trail (the actual midpoint is in the Pine Grove Furnace State Park in Pennsylvania, about seventy-five miles north of Harpers Ferry). There was something special about being in that place on that date. I wasn't going to let myself think that I was done, but if you added up all the miles I'd walked plus the 200 miles I'd aqua blazed, I'd traveled about 2,200 miles, the full length of the AT. But like I said, I wasn't going to start celebrating until I'd officially walked all of those miles, until I reached Glasgow.

But I would celebrate my birthday with some wine with a friend of my trail angel host, a flight attendant named Karen. We visited some local wineries near the Appalachian Mountains. Besides some great wine, one of the wineries gave me a birthday card. What an awesome day!

Celebrating my forty-first birthday with a trail angel at a winery

I had about 235 more miles left when my host dropped me off at the trail the next morning. I had trail angels lined up to take me into their homes for most of the next week, which really helped me focus on hiking. When I got close to Luray, I got a ride into town and stayed at a hiker hostel called the Open Arms at the Edge of Town. Alison, the owner of the hostel, drove me to and from the trail for the next several days, which allowed me to slackpack my way through a good chunk of the Shenandoah National Park. I really pushed myself. I had three twenty-mile days during that stretch, including a day when I hiked 24.4 miles. That's almost a full marathon! I was damn proud of that day. That's a good day for a person with two healthy legs, but for someone walking on a prosthetic leg, that's a day to brag about.

After three days of slackpacking, I was in the southern tip of Shenandoah National Park. I had about 75 miles left, and I felt good. I was making great time, and I was becoming giddy about nearly being done. I felt the same elation I'd experienced toward the end of my PCT hike. But I was also starting to feel a twinge of sadness. Hiking the AT had been my life for more than nine months, and I was going to miss the routine and the daily grind. I was also going to miss the generosity and emotional support of all the people who were doing so much for me along the trail. It's easy to get addicted to kindness from strangers.

I think I must have jinxed myself with all that anticipation about finishing my hike because I woke up in a lean-to shelter the next morning and discovered that my stump was horribly swollen. It looked like some twisted doctor had surgically implanted a baseball under my skin while I was sleeping. I really shouldn't have tried to walk on it, but I had no choice but to force the stump into the socket and push through the pain, which was excruciating. The night before, I'd made arrangements with some friends to meet outside of Shenandoah Park that day. I either had to put my leg on and limp six miles to the nearest trailhead or to throw my leg into my backpack and crawl.

My stump swelled to the size of a baseball after a week of intense hiking

Shitty shit! I felt like such a fool. I'd convinced myself that I was done struggling with my leg, that all the hardship was behind me. I was acting like I didn't have this disability. I was pushing my body the way I'd pushed it when I was hiking the PCT on two legs. I was practically inviting my stump to rebel to stop the abuse. I'd been intent on finishing before Christmas, which was less than two weeks away, but I'd treated my body so carelessly that I might have forced myself off the trail for weeks. I might not finish before the end of the year now. It could be even longer. What if I'd done so much damage this time that I had to stay off the trail for good? What if I couldn't finish?

"Pain makes you stronger.
Tears make you wiser.
Thank the past for a better future."
~ Marc

No, that wasn't going to happen. I wasn't going to let my disability defeat me. I'd have to take a little time off to recover, but I'd get back on the trail and finish what I started. Too many people had helped me get this far, and I wasn't about to disappoint them by quitting when I was so close. Hell, I'd crawl on my hands and knees to Glasgow if I had to. I was going to finish. Maybe it wouldn't be before the end of the year, but I'd definitely finish.

When I arrived at the trailhead, I kept walking along the Shenandoah Park's Scenic Road and stuck out my thumb. A park ranger who was driving the opposite direction stopped because my face was covered in tears. I asked him to take me out of the park, but he told me he wasn't allowed to give rides to hitchhikers. I couldn't believe it. Couldn't he see that I was in excruciating pain and walking on a prosthetic leg?

I limped along for another forty-five minutes before another car drove by. The driver was traveling north, but when I explained the situation, she told me that she was happy to turn around and drive me out of the park to the visitor center, which was only a few miles away. I finally had cell phone reception again when she dropped me off, and I called my friends.

When they arrived, and saw the pain written on my face, we decided that I should go straight to an emergency room in a hospital in Waynesboro. The doctor who examined me told me no surprise that I had an infection, and he prescribed rest and a ten-day course of antibiotics. I was relieved that the injury wasn't worse, but I was also angry at myself for putting myself in this situation. I'd pushed my body the way I'd pushed it when I had two legs, and now I had to take at least a week and a half off, which meant that there was no chance I'd finish before Christmas. I might not even finish before the end of the year. There's a fine line between courage and foolishness, and I'd crossed that line.

Hoping to cheer me up, my friends took me to a winery for a little grape therapy. A voice in my head wanted me to feel sorry for myself, but I refused to listen. This was just the latest in a series of minor setbacks. After the infection healed, I'd be back on the trail, and I'd finish what I started. I only had about 75 miles left until I reached Glasgow. I wouldn't let this stop me from getting to my final destination or from enjoying myself at the winery. In spite of the throbbing in my leg, my friends and I had a blast tasting those wines.

Wine tasting after a visit to the emergency room with the hikers I met at the Woods Hole Hostel

The day after my trip to the ER, my friends drove me all the way back up to the Open Arms at the Edge of Town Hostel in Luray. Everything south of Shenandoah Park was closed, so I had to recover in Luray. That was fine by me. Alison is a kind woman, and if I needed an extended stay to recover, I was happy to be in her presence.

But after more than a week on my butt, I was bored. I just wanted to get up and get back on the trail. I had a serious case of cabin fever, but the swelling hadn't subsided yet. The trail was calling my name, and it was maddening to ignore it while my stump healed. I also hated walking around on crutches. I desperately wanted to get back on the AT and finish what I started.

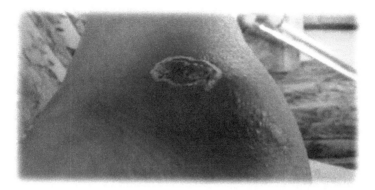

My stump after a week of rest

I posted an update on Facebook, explaining how miserable I was after being cooped up indoors for the past week, and a family that lived nearby replied with an invitation to dinner and to crash in their guest room. I accepted their offer, and I was soon in their kitchen cooking them some gluten-free Bubaspitzla, a Southern German dumpling whose name translates to "little boy penis." In spite of its name, it's a tasty dish, and I tried to make it as often as possible for my trail angels to thank them for their hospitality.

German dumpling whose name translates to "little boy penis"

A close-up shot of Bubaspitzla

I got another chance to thank them the next night, when I cooked for a dinner party at their friend's house. I made an Alaska salmon dish that got rave reviews from the guests. Most of the people at the party were AT enthusiasts, and several of them had been following my trek on Facebook. I received lots of encouraging words that night, and that made me eager to get back out there and finish.

After more than a week of recovery, my trail angels drove me back to the trailhead. I had about 75 miles to go. My leg was still sore, but it was infinitely better than it had been before going to the ER. That first day back on the trail was a good day, and I logged about fifteen miles. Toward the end of that day, a woman reached out to me on Facebook and offered to pick me up and take me to a brewery called the Devil's Backbone. She also invited me to stay at her house on my last few days on the trail. I often wondered while I was on the AT what hikers had done in the days before Facebook. I wouldn't have met half as many people on the AT if not for social media.

I spent Christmas Eve and Christmas Day on the trail, which wasn't as big a deal to me as it might have been to some people. Back when I was working as a chef in Europe, Christmas was always the busiest time of the year at the restaurants and in my own catering business, and I had to work the holiday just about every year. It was also nice not having to worry about buying a bunch of ridiculous gifts and eating way too much food. Not to mention that it was quiet on the AT, and I got to enjoy the trail in peace. Chatting with a hiking buddy is wonderful, but so is closing your mouth and opening your ears to the wild sounds of unpeopled places.

On my last few days on the trail, I started to think seriously about what I'd do after I finished, both in the short term and in the long term. Many of the people I'd met on the trail told me that my story was so inspirational that I should consider turning it into a book. That was a daunting thought when I first started toying with the idea, but the more I thought about it, the more appealing it seemed. If I wrote a book, it could encourage other amputees to get off the couch and get back to living. If I could hike the AT with a prosthetic leg, then so could a vet who lost a limb on a battlefield. It's easy to get bogged down in negative thoughts, especially if you're constantly getting told by family, friends, and doctors about the things you can't do anymore rather than all the things you still can do. If I could write something that could help people see the world and their place in it through a rosier set of lenses, then I would have accomplished something far more significant than my hike. Helping people rediscover their faith in themselves after a major setback would be awesome.

I thought I should start reaching out to people through local media outlets immediately after I finished. I called a couple local television stations and left messages saying I'd be in Glasgow in two days. If I gave some interviews at the end of my hike, I could post a link to it on my Facebook page, which still had thousands of pairs of eyes on it every day. It would be a good way to start touching lives.

I probably could have stayed at a trail angel's house during my last night on the AT, but I thought it was important to spend that final night outside on the trail, even if it was a cold, wet night that chilled my bones. I arrived at a shelter late that night, and the lean-to was packed full of snoring hikers who were escaping the rain. I had to hang my hammock on a pair of trees next to the shelter, and the little rain-fly I made over the hammock got drenched. It seemed fitting that my final night was so miserable. Even on that last leg of my hike, I had to push through adversity.

I thought my last day was going to be soggy and unpleasant, but the rain stopped in the earliest hours of the morning, and the sun shined brightly as I packed my backpack one last time. My leg was sore when I started hiking, but I didn't care. I felt wonderful. Everything seemed perfect. There weren't too many boulders or rocks in the way. There were no black flies to harass me or gusts of wind to blow me off the trail. It was the ideal day to finish my walk to recovery.

A couple days earlier, I'd posted an open invitation on Facebook to all my friends. I intended to jump off the bridge in Glasgow that crossed the James River, and I told everyone who was following me that they were welcome to join me. I doubted I'd get any takers on a plunge into the icy waters of the James in December, but I was curious to see if anyone would show up to celebrate with me.

My mind raced in those last couple hours before I arrived at Glasgow. Memories from the previous two years flooded my brain. Just twenty-six months earlier, I'd been lying at the bottom of a canyon, my body smashed, and my spirits battered. I thought I was dying that day in Utah, but my training as an athlete saved me. Then I started my long road to recovery. I'd been convinced back then that I was done with the life of adventure and exploration that had taken me to so many fascinating places and introduced me to countless intriguing people, and I didn't know what I'd do if I couldn't be out in the world, pushing my body to exhaustion and expanding my understanding of life. But like so many of my fears, reality didn't match up with the hell my mind had conjured up. If someone had told me while I was lying in that hospital in Colorado that I'd finish my hike on the AT just twenty-six months later, I would have told him to shove his cheery optimism where the sun don't shine. But here I was, about to walk the last of those 2,200 miles. My body had proven to me time and again that it's not what it used to be. I can't abuse it with impunity the way I did when I had two legs. But my spirit was so much stronger at the end of the AT than it had been in those days just after my accident. And maybe it was stronger than it had ever been. I've never considered myself mentally weak, but the person who lay in the hospital in Colorado and joked about suicide was not the same person who was about to cross the finish line.

"If you dream it, you can achieve it"
~ Zig Ziglar

I arrived at the bridge that marked the endpoint of my hike in the late afternoon. I was met by a local TV crew that had come to film my last steps and to interview me for the evening news. There were also a handful of other people who'd shown up to celebrate with me. A woman I'd met in Massachusetts came to tell me how much she admired me and how much my hike meant to her. A man brought a cooler full of beer and invited me to crash at his place that night. A mother came with her toddler strapped to her back to film me jumping into the river. It was a Sunday and the end of a long holiday weekend, and I was a little surprised that so many people had come, but I suppose I shouldn't have been. After all, I'd met dozens of trail angels in my nine and a half months on the AT.

With a small crowd of people clapping and cheering, I crossed the bridge over the James River. Then I threw my arms into the air and smiled.

I was done. My walk to recovery was finished.

EPILOGUE
ALWAYS PUSHING ON, NEVER GIVING UP

You might think that after being on the move for more than three-quarters of a year, I'd take some time to savor my accomplishment, to kick back and relax, but I've never been one to sit around relaxing (unless you count the time I spend in hot springs). The days that followed were a whirlwind. There was a TV studio interview at a local news station in Glasgow; a rental car road trip to Georgia to celebrate New Year's Eve with my friend Diane; a drive to Florida to pick up my motorcycle; a visit to a mechanic's garage to repair that stupid electronic hand shifter again; a quick test ride on my bike to Key West, including an overnight stay on a sailboat; a second visit to that mechanic's garage to replace that damn shifter with a manual shifter; a party with some Adventure Riders at Lake Charles, Louisiana; a trip to Big Bend National Park in Texas; a border crossing into Juarez, Mexico, to get my teeth fixed on the cheap; a radio interview in Ruidoso, New Mexico, where I once worked as a ski instructor; a drive to Truth or Consequences, New Mexico, to pick up my van from Jeffrey's place, where it had been sitting in the desert for almost two years; a thorough cleaning of the mess created by the mice that had taken residence in my van; a loading of my motorcycle onto the back of my van; and, finally, a drive up to Denver.

Not long after I got home, I started doing some research about writing a book that recounted my accident and my walk on the AT. I was determined to put my story down in words, but I didn't know where to start. I was brainstorming one morning about where to look for advice about writing my story when it occurred to me that I didn't need to look any further than my Facebook friends list. John, who'd helped me land that sponsorship deal with Adidas, has written more than forty books about his years of climbing and adventuring. He understands the life of the extreme athlete because he has lived that life for decades, and he's a writer who knows how to keep a reader turning pages. I reached out to him on Facebook, asking him what he recommended. He generously offered to fly out to Colorado to help me figure out how to turn my story into a book. A week later, I picked John up from the Denver airport, and we drove together in my van to my favorite hot springs at Valley View near Salida, Colorado. We spent a weekend there, and we put together an outline of my story. He did an awesome job painting it in broad brushstrokes to get me started. If he hadn't gone out of his way to come to Denver from LA, you wouldn't be reading the book you're holding right now.

Around that time, I started practicing rowing in a local club in the hope that I could qualify to compete in the Paralympics in Tokyo, Japan, in 2020. I was in great shape after hiking the AT, and I thought that this was the perfect time to make a push to achieve another dream. But injuries interfered yet again when I dislocated my right shoulder for the eleventh time.

The first dislocation happened in 2009 when I was in free fall while skydiving near Denver. After several months of physical therapy and regular swimming, I thought I was healed enough to skydive again, but I realized my mistake when it dislocated a second time while I was in free fall. The third time I heard that sickening click was when I was skiing while dragging an empty toboggan and carrying a bunch of bamboo poles during a training exercise as a ski patroller in 2010. After that, I went back to Germany to get orthoscopic surgery on my shoulder, and my arm was in a sling for months. The next time happened after I finished my AT hike, while I was indoor skydiving with some adaptive friends in Denver, and all that effort to go to Germany for surgery and rehab was wasted. A few days later, I dislocated my shoulder again, while I was sleeping. Then it popped out in physical therapy days after that. The seventh time happened while I was taking a rowing test to demonstrate my skills how to reenter the boat on the Lake. My rowing coach panicked the eighth time it dislocated, but I was a strong swimmer, and even with only one good arm and one good leg, I managed to make it safely to shore.

I ended up in the ER after every dislocation. My shoulder went into spasms each time, and the medical staff tried their best to put it back into its socket the conventional way, but they eventually gave up. They had to knock me out and use a muscle relaxer to pop it back in.

After an overnight stay in the hospital because they couldn't put the shoulder back in place, a surgeon who specializes in shoulders, Dr. S, recommended that I have surgery for a second time to repair all the ligaments. This time it would be an open shoulder operation, but he thought he could fix the problem once and for all.

I'd been reluctant to have yet another surgery, but after another couple dislocations, I finally agreed that it was time to get it taken care of it. You know it's time to take drastic measures when you dislocate your shoulder while you're sleeping! I went under the knife for nearly five hours, so the doctor could sew the ligaments back together. As far was shoulder surgeries go, it was major, but I was still released from the hospital that same day. That was fine by me. I've spent more than enough days in the hospital for one lifetime, and I was happy to get out as quickly as possible.

My recovery from surgery was painfully long, but I needed to let my shoulder heal properly so I wouldn't end up back in the operating room. I obviously had to give up any physical activity that would put undue strain on my shoulder. This was probably the ideal time for me to start my book. I needed to sit down and get to writing.

Using John's outline as my starting point, I wrote a couple chapters in the weeks that followed. I thought my story was engaging, but I knew I'd need help polishing my writing. Not only am I not a writer, but English is also my second language. I joined a writing club, thinking that I could get some direction and advice. Instead, I got a lot of criticism. I started having serious doubts about my ability to write a book. Who was I to think I could write something worth reading? To write a book, you have sit behind a desk for hours and hours at a time, but I'm addicted to physical activity. How could I sit still long enough to tell my story?

No, I couldn't give in to those negative thoughts. I'd push on, just as I had on the AT. I'd find a way to whip my words into shape. But it was probably best to take on the project somewhere other than Denver. I love the Mile-High City. I have dozens of friends there, and there are countless outdoor activities—not to mention breweries. Plus, my motorcycle, and the call of the open road is amplified whenever I'm within a stone's throw of my bike. And with winter coming, I'd be tempted to ski all season. I needed to get away from all those distractions. It was just a matter of figuring out where to go.

I got online and started doing some research about possible places to escape interruptions. I kicked around a couple ideas, but I eventually settled on Hawaii. My friend Bobby still lived on the Big Island, and he told me that I could crash on his couch whenever I wanted. So, I booked a one-way flight to Hilo, packed my bags, and took a plane to paradise.

To maintain the strength, I'd built on the AT, I signed up for yoga and spin classes at the University of Hawaii. The Hilo campus also offered an advanced scuba-dive class for a huge student discount, of which I took advantage. In addition, I swam in an Olympic-sized pool to rehab my shoulder. Then I got online to look for an editor who could help me tell my story. I found a guy named Jeremy Herman in Nevada, and after talking to him about my experiences, I felt confident I'd found the right person to help me write my story. We made a deal, sat down in our separate states, and got to work. I used John's outline to write the chapters, then I emailed them to Jeremy, so he could chisel off the rough edges of my English.

I'd be lying if I said I loved the writing process. Jeremy tells me that nothing makes him happier than sitting in front of a computer and typing away for hours at a stretch, but my idea of hell is a place where people are forced to sit in front of a computer and peck away at a keyboard all day. I need to be outside or in a gym, so I can get my body moving and my blood pumping. Writing this story was incredibly challenging for me, but I pushed on. I got into a routine, and little by little, the story started to come into focus. There were days when I thought I might quit—it seems like there were millions of them—but I reminded myself that I'd hiked the AT on a prosthetic leg just fourteen months after my fall in Utah. If I could do that, then I could get through this book as well.

About six months after I started working with Jeremy, I met a guy with a sailboat and a love of adventure. We quickly became friends, and I shared some of my stories with him. He said he was impressed with what I'd done over the years, and he invited me to sail with him to French Polynesia the following month.

I had about a month before he set sail to complete everything, but the reward waiting at the end of those weeks of intense labor would be an amazing journey. It would definitely be worth the effort, so I sat down at my laptop and pecked away at that keyboard. If I'm being honest, I hated that month, but I slogged through it and finished my story.

As the day of my departure approached, I started to feel that elation I always feel when I'm about to set off into the unknown. Some people love the sense of security that comes with routine but doing the same thing day after day is oppressive to me. What I love more than anything is waking up in the morning and not knowing where exactly I'm going to be when I go to sleep that night. There's always something new over the horizon, and all it takes is some effort to find out what it is.

I was looking forward for a new adventure when I jumped on my bicycle with my gear the day we were scheduled to depart. I was looking forward to sleeping on the ocean that night. But before I could board that boat, disaster struck.

I was cycling through downtown Hilo when I started feeling dizzy, probably due to dehydration caused by the massage I got for my shoulder an hour earlier. I was already a little wobbly when a blast of wind hit me and my bicycle. I have click pedals, and the salt water in the air had made them a little rusty, so it was difficult to snap my feet out. When the wind hit me, I couldn't get my shoe unlocked from the pedal, and I fell hard on my left side.

A woman stopped to help me. I was lying face down, trying to get up, telling myself that I was fine. But an intense pain shot up from my left leg, and I realized that something was seriously wrong. Shitty shit!

Someone else arrived at the scene of the accident and called the ambulance. The paramedics offered me morphine, but I refused because I was trying to convince myself that this was a minor injury. I had to wait at the hospital for a couple hours before I got an x-ray. When the doctor came in carrying the results, he asked me if I wanted some pain meds now. I asked him why, and he held up the x-ray, wounding my optimism and bruising my adventurous spirit.

The neck of my femur was broken, and I was bleeding internally. I needed immediate surgery. As soon as I signed a consent form, I was rolled into the operating room yet again.

Lying in a hospital after surgery, even more "screwed up" than ever before, I was really upset that I wouldn't be able to set sail with the crew that day. I could have just given up on the opportunity to sail to French Polynesia, but I that's not my style. Push on: that's my style.

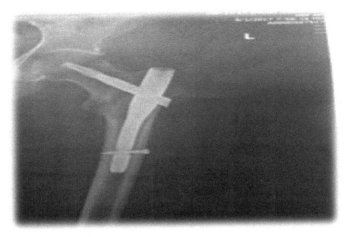

All screwd up after surgery on my femur

It was going to take the ship more than thirty days to sail from Hawaii to Tahiti, so I decided that I'd get healthy and meet them there, which was exactly what I did. I pushed myself through my own course of physical therapy, and in four weeks I was healed enough to walk without crutches. I took a plane to Tahiti, where I met up with the captain and the crew. I spent the next couple weeks scuba diving in one of the best places in the world.

Saying goodbye to the crew as they left Hawaii

The highlight of my sailing experience was a drift dive, where your body is carried underwater by the push of the tide. The current is strong, and it moves you quite fast. When you scuba dive, you feel weightless as you float. It's almost the same sensation as skydiving. After dislocating my shoulder too many times, I had to give up skydiving, the only sport I can't do any more. But here I was in French Polynesia, "skydiving" sixty feet underwater, moving at twelve knots (about fourteen miles per hour). I even saw a lemon shark floating by, smiling at me with its razor-sharp teeth.

What a day! As I always say:

"Never give up in life,
because you never know
what's around the corner.
Always push on."
~ Niki Rellon

Scuba Diving with Lemon sharks in French Polynesia

ABOUT THE AUTHOR

Niki Rellon is a trained chef, paramedic, boxing and kickboxing champion, ski instructor, and motivational speaker, among other things. She's also the first woman to have hiked the Appalachian Trail, from Georgia to Maine, on a prosthetic leg.

Born in Germany, Niki became a US citizen and immersed herself completely in American culture. She has cycled from Alaska to Mexico City and has ridden her motorcycle across the continent multiple times.

While she was rappelling in Utah in 2013, Niki suffered a traumatic fall that left her with horrific injuries, including a broken pelvis and spine. And her left foot was so badly damaged that it had to be amputated.

This would have meant the end of extreme sports for some, but for Niki it meant new challenges. Against all advice, she decided to hike the Appalachian Trail with only a set of hiking poles, her new prosthetic leg, and bags of determination.

Niki's memoir, *Push On: My Walk to Recovery on the Appalachian Trail*, tells the story of courage and resolve. Her journey will inspire you to never give in, even when it seems like you're facing impossible odds.

Niki hasn't let her injury define her, and she continues to participate in numerous sports.

You can email her at nikirellon@gmail.com, contact her on Facebook, or visit her website at www.nikirellon.com.

"A memoir should have some uplifting quality, inspiring or illuminating, and that's what separates a life story that can influence other people.

~ Mitch Albom